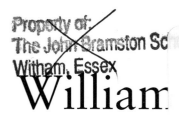

D0352466

William

Selected Works

◆

Edited by David Stevens

Series Editor: Judith Baxter

The publishers would like to thank Nicholas McGuinn and
Jane Ogborn for their help as consulting editors for the series.

Published by the Press Syndicate of the University of Cambridge
The Pitt Building, Trumpington Street, Cambridge CB2 1RP
40 West 20th Street, New York, NY 10011-4211, USA
10 Stamford Road, Oakleigh, Melbourne 3166, Australia

First published 1995

Printed in Great Britain by Scotprint, Musselburgh, Scotland

A catalogue record for this book is available from the British Library

ISBN 0 521 485460 paperback

Illustrations on pages 85–98 reproduction by permission of the Syndics
of the Fitzwilliam Museum, Cambridge; page 99 copyright British
Museum; page 100 courtesy of Tate Gallery, London.

Prepared for publication by Stenton Associates

CONTENTS

✦

CAMBRIDGE LITERATURE

This edition of selected writings of William Blake is part of the Cambridge Literature series, and has been specially prepared for students in schools and colleges who are studying Blake as part of their English course.

This study edition invites you to think about what happens when you read a poem, and it suggests that you are not passively responding to words on the page which have only one agreed interpretation, but that you are actively exploring and making *new* sense of what you read. Your 'reading' will partly stem from you as an individual, from your own experiences and point of view, and to this extent your interpretation will be distinctively your own. But your reading will also stem from the fact that you belong to a culture and a community, rooted in a particular time and place. So, your understanding may have much in common with that of others in your class or study group.

There is a parallel between the way you read this book and the way the poems came about. The Resource Notes at the back are devised to help you to investigate the complex nature of the writing process. This begins with the poet's first, tentative ideas and sources of inspiration, moves through to the stages of writing, production and publication, and ends with the text's reception by the reading public, reviewers, critics and students. So the general approach to study focuses on five key questions:

Who has written these poems and why?
What type of texts are they?
How were they produced?
How do they present their subject?
Who reads them? How do they interpret them?

The poems are presented complete and uninterrupted. Unfamiliar words and ideas are explained in the commentary.

The Resource Notes encourage you to take an active and imaginative approach to studying poetry both in and out of the classroom. As well as providing you with information about many aspects of Blake's work, they offer a wide choice of activities to work on individually, or in groups. Above all, they give you the chance to explore this intriguing writer in a variety of ways: as a reader, an actor, a researcher, a critic, and a writer.

Judith Baxter

INTRODUCTION

The reputation of William Blake, poet, painter, engraver and philosopher, has grown enormously over the past half century. Inevitably, so has the mass of critical material about his works. And yet, for all his complexity, it seems to me there remains an incisive simplicity in Blake's work which is refreshing and perennially appropriate.

My intentions in presenting a selection of Blake's work in this book are several. First, I should like to communicate some of my own sometimes obsessive enthusiasm for Blake – an enthusiasm sharpened by some of the excellent work undertaken by various English students at Samuel Ward Upper School in Haverhill, Helena Romanes School in Dunmow, and, latterly, Thirsk School. My enthusiasm for the teaching of Blake, as distinct from simply reading him, is founded on two premises: his work is accessible, and it is robust. You will need to work hard, but you will be rewarded – because a work is complex does not mean it is unapproachable or unclear. Perhaps Blake's robustness has something to do with it – such is the stature of the man's work that you can do almost anything to it, even irreverently, and it will still bounce back, all the better for the exercise. In the end this increases my respect for Blake, and it underpins many of the approaches and activities I have included here. There are five central questions regarding Blake which are certainly implicit or explicit in each approach; they are:

Who was Blake and why did he write these poems?
What type of texts are these poems and engravings?
How were the poems produced?
How does Blake present his various themes?
Who reads Blake's work and how is it interpreted?

In effect, these questions are the tools with which you can begin to grasp the complex and inspiring meanings of the man's life work.

The relationship between innocence and experience is fundamental to understanding Blake, and I have tried in this selection to relate everything to it, if only to give some sort of further unity of approach. It is possible to 'dip into' this book, just as it is possible to look only at one or two of Blake's poems and still derive immense satisfaction. Nevertheless, I suggest that deeper understanding comes with more complete knowledge, and is incremental; this selection is based on a growing awareness and is best read in sequence. The approaches and activities vary in type and complexity: some are theoretical, others more practical; some aim to establish a basic familiarity, whilst others should lead you to a deeper understanding. Ideally, try to experience a balance between these options in the Activities and Approaches sections for the poems you are studying, having first read the poem at least once and considered the initial questions. For ease of access, spelling has been modernised.

This is only a small selection of Blake's work, but it may lead to an exploration of his total art. For there is unity in Blake; there are many parts – many more than we think, perhaps – and yet there is a wholeness which I hope will emerge with increasing clarity. Perhaps, too, there is a holiness – but you yourself must be the judge of that.

David Stevens

Songs of Innocence and of Experience

The 'Songs of Innocence' were originally published by William Blake in the momentous year of 1789 as an engraved book in its own right, although he had been working on the poems for some years and several had had a place in his satirical 'An Island in the Moon' of about 1787. The idea of writing a complementary, or contrasting, collection of poems dealing with experience seems to have come to Blake fairly soon afterwards, and there is evidence that he was working on them in the early 1790s. It was not until 1794, however, that he added the poems of experience to the earlier volume, with the title *Songs of Innocence and of Experience*; the 'Experience' poems were never published separately. During the five years, Blake was working at different times on the illustrations, and it is quite possible that he was writing 'Experience' poems while illustrating 'Innocence'; certainly, the two 'states of the human soul' were very closely linked in Blake's mind, and there are several changes in the composition of each part and in the designs of the illustrations to underline this.

✦ *Activities*

1 Explore the nature of the words 'innocence' and 'experience' in everyday life. What associations does each have, both positive and negative? Note that Blake was writing within a pastoral tradition where 'innocence' was virtually a cliché; he was concerned to transform its stale meaning through his poetry. Experience could be viewed as an inevitable and healthy growth towards a sense of the world's often harsh reality, or more negatively as the destruction of openness and spontaneity. There is evidence for both; certainly, by 1797, Blake was writing:

> What is the price of Experience? Do men buy it for a song?
> Or wisdom for a dance in the street? No, it is bought with the price
> Of all that a man hath, his houses, his wife, his children
> > (Night Two of *Vala* or *The Four Zoas*)

2 What is the effect of the subtitle 'Showing the Contrary States of the Human Soul'? Is harmony or discord suggested?

'Introduction' to 'The Songs of Innocence'

A true introduction to the 'Songs of Innocence', this first poem in the book, brings together a piper and a child in happy partnership, located in a setting of rural bliss, with the child apparently calling the tune.

- Who is the piper representing? And the lamb?
- How does he or she broadcast the message?
- Why does the child vanish? Where to?
- What happens when the piper starts writing? Do any problems arise?
- To whom is the poem primarily addressed: children or adults?

✦ *Activities and approaches*

1 Arrange a group reading of the poem, taking the two parts in choral style. Try echoing the words suggesting **joy** to emphasise the mood. If possible, use music to create a song.

2 Imagine and write the script of the child reporting the incident to (possibly) doubtful parents: what would they think or say? Would suspicion come into it?

'The Shepherd'

Now the shepherd adds detail to the pastoral picture, and the poem seems to emphasise the wise, caring relationship with the flock.

- Is there any direct continuity from 'The Introduction'?
- There are clear Biblical echoes. Look at Psalm 23 for comparison. What do you make of this comparison?
- Why 'strays' (l. 2)? Does this word suggest neglect of duty?
- An ancient Zen Buddhist saying states that the way to control a flock of sheep is to give them a wide area to wander in: is this the attitude of the shepherd here? Can you relate this to wider areas of control and authority in society?
- To whom is the shepherd offering 'praise' (l. 4)? Why?

✦ *Activities and approaches*

1 Imagine you are the shepherd and write a description of your role, showing your attitude to the work and mentioning also the relationship with any higher authority or employer.

2 Explore the word 'pastoral' as used above. Why do schools have 'pastoral systems'? What does Beethoven's 'Pastoral Symphony' signify? Why are Church clerics known as Pastors?

You might conduct further research into the 'pastoral tradition' of English poetry, within which Blake was working.

Introduction

Piping down the valleys wild,
Piping songs of pleasant glee,
On a cloud I saw a child,
And he laughing said to me:

'Pipe a song about a lamb.'   5
So I piped with merry cheer.
'Piper, pipe that song again.'
So I piped; he wept to hear.

'Drop thy pipe, thy happy pipe;
Sing thy songs of happy cheer.'   10
So I sung the same again,
While he wept with joy to hear.

'Piper sit thee down and write
In a book that all may read –'
So he vanished from my sight.   15
And I plucked a hollow reed,

And I made a rural pen,
And I stained the water clear,
And I wrote my happy songs
Every child may joy to hear.   20

The Shepherd

How sweet is the shepherd's sweet lot!
From the morn to the evening he strays;
He shall follow his sheep all the day,
And his tongue shall be filled with praise.

For he hears the lamb's innocent call,   5
And he hears the ewe's tender reply.
He is watchful, while they are in peace,
For they know when their shepherd is nigh.

'The Echoing Green'

The poem clearly shows children being gently cared for by adults, and enjoying the freedom of unrestricted play. The adults seem to be kind and benevolent, remembering their own childhoods and responding happily to the children.

- Who is the narrator here? Compare with the previous poems.
- How does the rhythm alter from the other poems? Why is there this change? Note the pairs of unstressed syllables, and the swift repetition of the rhymes.
- Why is this an 'echoing' setting? What is echoing what? Does it have any symbolic significance for the relationships mentioned?
- Which new elements of nature are introduced? What associations do they convey to you?
- Is the adult–child relationship the same as the one between shepherd and flock or piper and child?
- The poem ends with 'the darkening green' (l. 30). What significance has this, do you think?

✦ *Activities and approaches*

1 In pairs, interview Old John on his memories of childhood.

2 Give a performance of the poem with appropriate sound effects, using keyboards if possible, to emphasise the atmosphere. In this reading, aim to show how the mood of the poem changes, and experiment with different kinds of mood.

The Echoing Green

The sun does arise,
And make happy the skies.
The merry bells ring
To welcome the spring.
The skylark and thrush,   5
The birds of the bush,
Sing louder around,
To the bells' cheerful sound,
While our sports shall be seen
On the echoing green.   10

Old John with white hair
Does laugh away care,
Sitting under the oak,
Among the old folk.
They laugh at our play,   15
And soon they all say:
'Such, such were the joys
When we all, girls and boys,
In our youth-time were seen
On the echoing green.'   20

Till the little ones weary
No more can be merry;
The sun does descend,
And our sports have an end.
Round the laps of their mothers   25
Many sisters and brothers,
Like birds in their nest,
Are ready for rest;
And sport no more seen
On the darkening green.   30

'The Blossom'

There is an evocative atmosphere of innocence here, with imagery drawn from the natural world, but it is precisely this imagery which perhaps leads us away from the innocent world we have so far witnessed.

- Describe what is happening in the illustration on page 85. Does this help your understanding of the poem?
- What do you think the blossom, the sparrow, and the robin signify? Are they appropriate symbols? What, for example, do you know of the behaviour and appearance of either bird, in reality or in nursery rhyme tradition?
- Who is the narrator here?
- Why is the blossom apparently happy, whilst the robin is 'sobbing, sobbing' (l. 10)? How does it fit into the world of innocence?
- Do you consider any of the images in the poem to be particularly male or female? Is your understanding of the poem affected by your answer here?

✦ *Activity*

Prepare a mimed performance of the poem in small groups, emphasising and experimenting with different meanings through your imaginative use of body language while one or more of the group reads the poem aloud.

The Blossom

Merry, merry sparrow,
Under leaves so green,
A happy blossom
Sees you swift as arrow
Seek your cradle narrow   5
Near my bosom.

Pretty, pretty robin,
Under leaves so green,
A happy blossom
Hears you sobbing, sobbing,   10
Pretty, pretty robin
Near my bosom.

'The Lamb'

Here, clearly, there is a resumption of the pastoral imagery of 'The Shepherd', with all its Biblical connotations. The poem is based around a series of gentle recurring questions and, in the second stanza, answers and affirmations.

- Who is the speaker here?
- What is the Biblical significance of the lamb and the child?
- What is being affirmed in the second stanza, and by whom?
- Who is the 'he' of the second stanza? Why is the child 'called by his name' (l. 18)? In what sense did he become 'a little child' (l. 16)?
- What might a modern young child, perhaps from an urban background, make of this poem? You could perhaps read it to younger brothers or sisters, noting the effect.

✦ *Activity*

Imagine and then recount the thoughts of the lamb itself on being confronted by this questioner. Might the lamb's thoughts and possible answers differ from those of the poem's narrator?

The Lamb

Little Lamb who made thee?
Dost thou know who made thee?
Gave thee life and bid thee feed
By the stream and o'er the mead;
  Gave thee clothing of delight,   5
  Softest clothing woolly bright;
  Gave thee such a tender voice,
    Making all the vales rejoice.
  Little Lamb who made thee?
Dost thou know who made thee?   10

    Little Lamb I'll tell thee,
    Little Lamb I'll tell thee:
  He is callèd by thy name,
  For he calls himself a lamb.
  He is meek and he is mild;   15
  He became a little child.
  I a child and thou a lamb,
  We are callèd by his name.
  Little Lamb God bless thee.
  Little Lamb God bless thee.   20

'Laughing Song'

Here is a vision of happy innocence involving children – who are for the first time in *Songs of Innocence and of Experience* actually named. They have realistic English names rather than the idealised names Edessa, Lyca and Emilie which Blake used for a previous version of the poem in his earlier collection 'Poetical Sketches'.

- Which of the previous poems is this one most like?
- Who is the speaker here – a child or an adult? How does your answer affect your understanding of the poem?
- While reading the poem aloud, consider the rhythm carefully. Does it suggest the innocence theme in any way?
- Why are the birds 'painted' (l. 9)? Does the idea of painted birds fit in with the vision of natural innocence? Think of stories or fairy tales involving painted and real birds.
- Consider the nature of laughter. Do we, for example, often laugh when by ourselves? How do your thoughts affect your reading of the poem?

✦ *Activities and approaches*

1 Blake sang many of the 'Songs of Innocence' to his small but apparently appreciative audience. This poem is perhaps most obviously a song. Aim to set it and perform it to your own music.

2 Design a collage of photographs and pictures on the theme of laughter and childhood fun, using the poem itself as the centrepiece of the whole design.

Laughing Song

When the green woods laugh with the voice of joy
And the dimpling stream runs laughing by,
When the air does laugh with our merry wit
And the green hill laughs with the noise of it,

When the meadows laugh with lively green   5
And the grasshopper laughs in the merry scene,
When Mary and Susan and Emily
With their sweet round mouths sing 'Ha, Ha, He,'

When the painted birds laugh in the shade
Where our table with cherries and nuts is spread –   10
Come live and be merry and join with me,
To sing the sweet chorus of 'Ha, Ha, He.'

'The Little Black Boy'

This poem, perhaps for the first time in the 'Songs of Innocence', acknowledges a problem in the idyllic world presented: people, even children, do not always get an even chance in life. Blake, moving in politically radical circles, was painfully aware of the harsh realities of slavery at a time when the anti-slavery campaign was gaining ground. The poem itself, spoken as if by a black child, repays careful study, as its possible meanings are far from straightforward.

- Is the first stanza a lament? How else could it be read?
- What meaning may the word 'bereaved' (l. 4) have? How close is it to the word 'bereft'?
- Put into your own words the mother's comforting argument. How convincing do you find it?
- What do you understand by 'bear the beams of love' (l. 14)?
- Whose voice will apparently be heard in the fifth stanza?
- What might the black and white clouds (l. 23) signify?
- Does the last stanza suggest that black and white boys will, in the end, be equal? Try reading it for opposing meanings.
- What is the effect of the first person narrative style?
- Do you consider the poem to be anti-racist, or does it in some way condone white supremacy?

✦ *Activities and approaches*

1 Consider whether a very young child would be aware of differences in colour and race, and what might have happened to the little black boy to lead up to this conversation with his mother. Discuss how this fits in with the world of Innocence, if at all.

2 List the associations of the words **black** and **white** in all kinds of contexts. How does this list help your understanding?

3 In small groups, conduct interviews of the key figures: the little black boy, his mother, the English boy, and Blake himself, in order to arrive at a clear meaning for the poem.

4 Using the library and any other available resources, research the history of slavery. Present your findings with the poem as an integral part.

The Little Black Boy

My mother bore me in the southern wild,
And I am black, but oh! my soul is white.
White as an angel is the English child;
But I am black as if bereaved of light.

My mother taught me underneath a tree,   5
And sitting down before the heat of day
She took me on her lap and kissèd me,
And pointing to the east began to say:

'Look on the rising sun! There God does live,
And gives his light and gives his heat away;   10
And flowers and trees and beasts and men receive
Comfort in morning, joy in the noon day.

'And we are put on earth a little space,
That we may learn to bear the beams of love;
And these black bodies and this sun-burnt face   15
Is but a cloud, and like a shady grove.

'For when our souls have learned the heat to bear
The cloud will vanish; we shall hear his voice,
Saying: "Come out from the grove my love and care,
And round my golden tent like lambs rejoice." '   20

Thus did my mother say and kissèd me,
And thus I say to little English boy.
When I from black and he from white cloud free,
And round the tent of God like lambs we joy,

I'll shade him from the heat till he can bear   25
To lean in joy upon our father's knee,
And then I'll stand and stroke his silver hair
And be like him, and he will then love me.

'The Chimney-Sweeper'

As in 'The Little Black Boy', a problem is presented – this time the misery of child labour in England. London, rapidly expanding into a chaotic metropolis, offered unscrupulous employers vast opportunities for exploitation of children, who, filthy, brutalised and suffering the most appalling injuries and diseases, were objects of fear among 'respectable' citizens. It took until 1875, well after Blake's death, for the law to prohibit such cruelty, but the poem continues to have a direct and disturbing relevance for many parts of the world even today.

- Compare the 'lamb' imagery (l. 6) to other poems. Does it have ominous overtones here? Read Isaiah 53:7 in the Bible.
- 'sold' (l. 2) refers to the actual practice of selling children into virtual slavery. Is there bitterness or acceptance here?
- 'weep …' (l. 3) is the street cry 'sweep!' poignantly abbreviated. How does it affect you as reader here?
- 'shaved' (l. 6) refers to the practice of shaving hair to ease access to the narrowest chimneys. What might this symbolise?
- What is the 'duty' (l. 24) and how is this ironic?
- Discuss the poem's ambiguities, centring on the key words 'free', 'good', 'want', 'joy', 'duty' and 'harm'.

✦ *Activities and approaches*

1 Discuss the presentation of light and darkness in the poem, comparing it to 'The Little Black Boy'.

2 Consider why Blake included the poem in 'Songs of Innocence'.

3 Present reasoned arguments advocating the poem as either a revolutionary call to action, or a plea to make the best of a bad job and accept suffering inflicted on us by others.

4 Write and present the dialogue between the Chimney-Sweeper and the 'Little Black Boy' of that poem, showing how their experiences and solutions would relate to each other.

The Chimney-Sweeper

When my mother died I was very young,
And my father sold me while yet my tongue
Could scarcely cry, 'weep weep weep weep'.
So your chimneys I sweep and in soot I sleep.

There's little Tom Dacre, who cried when his head,   5
That curled like a lamb's back, was shaved, so I said:
'Hush Tom, never mind it, for when your head's bare,
You know that the soot cannot spoil your white hair.'

And so he was quiet, and that very night,
As Tom was a-sleeping, he had such a sight: 10
That thousands of sweepers, Dick, Joe, Ned and Jack,
Were all of them locked up in coffins of black,

And by came an angel who had a bright key,
And he opened the coffins and set them all free.
Then down a green plain leaping, laughing they run,   15
And wash in a river and shine in the sun.

Then naked and white, all their bags left behind,
They rise upon clouds, and sport in the wind.
And the angel told Tom if he'd be a good boy,
He'd have God for his father and never want joy.   20

And so Tom awoke, and we rose in the dark,
And got with our bags and our brushes to work.
Though the morning was cold, Tom was happy and warm.
So if all do their duty, they need not fear harm.

'The Little Boy Lost' and 'The Little Boy Found'

A child's – perhaps universal – nightmare is described here: the child's security is threatened by his father's lack of communication, despite increasingly urgent pleas, and subsequent apparent disappearance. But because this is the world of innocence, harmony is restored: God and the father become one, reuniting the child with his mother.

- How do the two illustrations, on pages 86 and 87, help your understanding of the poems? Describe what you see.
- Does the father actually disappear? If so, why?
- What happens when the child weeps?
- Is the overall tone of the poems one of happiness or not?

✦ *Activities and approaches*

1 What significance do you find in the fact that the child, the parent and God are all male, whilst it is to the mother that the boy is eventually returned for comfort? Explore the gender roles as expressed in the poem, considering whether altered genders would change the poem's impact.

2 Imagining this to be a dream sequence, mime the events recounted.

3 Imagine that the child and parents are discussing the incident afterwards. Script what they would say to each other.

The Little Boy Lost

'Father, father where are you going?
Oh do not walk so fast.
Speak father, speak to your little boy,
Or else I shall be lost.'

The night was dark, no father was there,   5
The child was wet with dew.
The mire was deep, and the child did weep,
And away the vapour flew.

The Little Boy Found

The little boy lost in the lonely fen,
Led by the wand'ring light,
Began to cry, but God ever nigh
Appeared like his father in white.

He kissed the child and by the hand led,   5
And to his mother brought,
Who in sorrow pale through the lonely dale
Her little boy weeping sought.

'Holy Thursday'

This poem refers to the annual service at St. Paul's Cathedral on Maundy Thursday, traditionally the day of charity, for the London charity schools children, most of whom were abandoned orphans, and seems to celebrate the power of good in pity and charity. But there are certain questions here, as in so many of these innocent visions.

- How do the children walk, and what do they wear? How does this contrast with the descriptions of children freely playing in other 'Songs'? What does the rhythm suggest to you?
- What do the 'wands' (l. 3) suggest: kindness, magic or coercion?
- Is it significant that the poem is located in London? Are the 'flowers' (l. 5) somehow urban?
- The 'beadles' (l. 3) are the officials in charge of the children. What irony is there in showing them as 'wise guardians'? In what sense are they 'beneath' (l. 11) the children?

✦ Activities and approaches

1 Research the Biblical significance of the 'multitudes of lambs' (l. 7). Are there innocent and ominous associations here? Look at Matthew 14:19 in the Bible. Consider also Blake's views on the emotion of pity, referring to other writings, pictures and Hebrews 13:2 in the Bible.

2 Contrast, and choose a way of presenting, the inner thoughts and moods of the children and the beadles. Does either reflect the narrator's clearly pious view of the occasion?

3 Find and play appropriate music to accompany a performance of the poem.

Holy Thursday

'Twas on a Holy Thursday, their innocent faces clean,
The children walking two and two in red and blue and green,
Grey headed beadles walked before with wands as white as snow;
Till into the high dome of Paul's they like Thames waters flow.

Oh what a multitude they seemed, these flowers of London town. 5
Seated in companies they sit, with radiance all their own.
The hum of multitudes was there, but multitudes of lambs:
Thousands of little boys and girls raising their innocent hands.

Now like a mighty wind they raise to Heaven the voice of song,
Or like harmonious thunderings the seats of Heaven among. 10
Beneath them sit the agèd men, wise guardians of the poor.
Then cherish pity, lest you drive an angel from your door.

'A Cradle Song'

This poem is one of gentle mother–child intimacy, sensuous in its tone.

- Much of the poem appeals directly to the senses. Make a note of the various ways in which this is done, and the various senses implied. Do you find this very sensuous quality at all disturbing?
- Why does the infant need a 'shade' (l. 1)? Look again at 'The Little Black Boy'.
- Why is the word 'beguiles' (l. 12) used? Does it fit the innocent mood?
- Who is 'Thy maker' (l. 24)? Are God and the child's father somehow linked here? What is the mother's relationship to him? Are there similar links in other poems?

✦ *Activities and approaches*

1 In small groups, read the poem aloud with the sensuous words being echoed by extra voices.

2 Would this poem be a good lullaby? Look at and compare some other lullabies you may have heard, considering what elements are generally present in a lullaby.

A Cradle Song

Sweet dreams, form a shade
O'er my lovely infant's head,
Sweet dreams of pleasant streams,
By happy, silent, moony beams.

Sweet sleep, with soft down   5
Weave thy brows an infant crown.
Sweet sleep, angel mild,
Hover o'er my happy child.

Sweet smiles in the night,
Hover over my delight.   10
Sweet smiles, mother's smiles,
All the livelong night beguiles.

Sweet moans, dovelike sighs,
Chase not slumber from thy eyes.
Sweet moans, sweeter smiles,   15
All the dovelike moans beguiles.

Sleep, sleep happy child.
All creation slept and smiled.
Sleep, sleep, happy sleep,
While o'er thee thy mother weep.   20

Sweet babe, in thy face,
Holy image I can trace.
Sweet babe, once like thee
Thy maker lay, and wept for me,

Wept for me, for thee, for all,   25
When he was an infant small.
Thou his image ever see,
Heavenly face that smiles on thee,

Smiles on thee, on me, on all,
Who became an infant small.
Infant smiles are his own smiles;
Heaven and earth to peace beguiles.   30

'The Divine Image'

Idealised humanity is the theme of this poem, in the sense that, for Blake, God represents human spirituality at its most profound, rather than being an external or independent entity. This was a controversial, even sacrilegious, belief in the late eighteenth century, but it is absolutely central to Blake's view of humanity.

- Look closely at the verse patterns of the poem. How do they help in understanding the meaning?
- Is there any ambiguity in the line 'Pity a human face' (l. 10)? How can the meaning of the whole poem be altered by an alternative reading of this line?

✦ *Activities and approaches*

1 Give your own definitions of the central characteristics of 'Mercy, Pity, Peace and Love' (l. 1), showing how your own views relate to those expressed by Blake in this poem.

2 Imagine you are a cynical politician, and deliver your response to the views of the poem, perhaps as a letter to Blake.

3 Use the last stanza as a quotation in a short political speech, emphasising the idea of universal humanity. The 'heathen, Turk or Jew' (l. 18) represented for Blake examples of religious belief other than Christianity.

The Divine Image

To Mercy, Pity, Peace and Love
  All pray in their distress,
And to these virtues of delight
  Return their thankfulness.

For Mercy, Pity, Peace and Love   5
  Is God our father dear,
And Mercy, Pity, Peace and Love
  Is Man his child and care.

For Mercy has a human heart,
  Pity a human face,   10
And Love the human form divine,
  And Peace the human dress.

Then every man of every clime
  That prays in his distress,
Prays to the human form divine: 15
  Love, Mercy, Pity, Peace.

And all must love the human form,
  In heathen, Turk or Jew.
Where Mercy, Love and Pity dwell,
  There God is dwelling too.   20

'Night'

Innocence is afforded protection against the potential threats of darkness and night. There is cruelty in nature as well as in the human society of slavery and child labour, and in this poem an innocent, harmonious response is offered.

- Who is the speaker here? Is he or she an adult or a child? Is there any significance in the 'Farewell' (l. 9) to the joys of daytime?
- What are the angels actually doing? Describe how the threatening wild animals are pacified.
- Examine the Biblical significance of 'New worlds to inherit' (l. 32), and of the lion lying down with the lamb in apparent harmony (ll. 41–2). Look at Isaiah 2:6 particularly.
- Research also the baptismal imagery of 'life's river' (l. 45) – refer to Revelations 22:1–2 – and compare with other mentions of rivers and bathing in Blake's poetry.

✦ *Activities and approaches*

1 Imagine you are directing a short film which presents the poem; draw 'storyboard' sketches for each of the scenes.

2 Re-write the poem as a children's story, illustrated.

Night

The sun descending in the west,
The evening star does shine.
The birds are silent in their nest,
And I must seek for mine.
The moon, like a flower   5
In heaven's high bower,
With silent delight
Sits and smiles on the night.

Farewell green fields and happy groves,
Where flocks have took delight;   10
Where lambs have nibbled, silent moves
The feet of angels bright.

Unseen they pour blessing,
And joy without ceasing,
On each'bud and blossom,   15
And each sleeping bosom.

They look in every thoughtless nest,
Where birds are covered warm;
They visit caves of every beast,
To keep them all from harm.   20
If they see any weeping
That should have been sleeping,
They pour sleep on their head
And sit down by their bed.

When wolves and tigers howl for prey   25
They pitying stand and weep,
Seeking to drive their thirst away,
And keep them from the sheep.
But if they rush dreadful,
The angels most heedful,   30
Receive each mild spirit,
New worlds to inherit.

And there the lion's ruddy eyes
Shall flow with tears of gold,
And pitying the tender cries   35
And walking round the fold,
Saying: 'Wrath by his meekness,
And by his health sickness,
Is driven away
From our immortal day.   40

'And now beside thee, bleating lamb,
I can lie down and sleep,
Or think on him who bore thy name,
Graze after thee and weep.
For washed in life's river,   45
My bright mane for ever
Shall shine like the gold,
As I guard o'er the fold.'

'Spring'

A celebratory poem: the innocent joys of Spring are expressed through the imagery of childhood and nature.

- How does the rhythm of the poem emphasise the mood?
- The 'little boy' and the 'little girl' (ll. 10–14) are described differently. Is there any significance here?
- Do the descriptions of the boy and girl imply an adult speaker?

✦ *Activity*

Present this poem as a song, perhaps as a round: that is, sung by several voices, each singer taking up a line of the song in succession.

Spring

Sound the flute!
Now it's mute.
Birds delight
Day and night.
Nightingale   5
In the dale,
Lark in sky,
Merrily,
Merrily, merrily to welcome in the year.

Little boy   10
Full of joy.
Little girl
Sweet and small.
Cock does crow,
So do you.   15
Merry voice,
Infant noise,
Merrily, merrily to welcome in the year.

Little lamb
Here I am.   20
Come and lick
My white neck.
Let me pull
Your soft wool.
Let me kiss   25
Your soft face,
Merrily, merrily we welcome in the year.

'Nurse's Song'

In this poem, the children's nurse is guided by their wishes: she allows them to remain playing until tiredness sets in, although there just may be a certain reluctance in her attitude.

- Look closely at the language of the poem, particularly the rhythm, and the rather vague location. What mood is emphasised?

◆ *Activity*

Write the inner thoughts of the nurse, perhaps contrasting the negative with the positive as she reflects on the children.

Nurse's Song

When the voices of children are heard on the green
And laughing is heard on the hill,
My heart is at rest within my breast
And everything else is still.

'Then come home my children: the sun is gone down   5
And the dews of night arise.
Come, come leave off play and let us away,
Till the morning appears in the skies.'

'No, no let us play, for it is yet day
And we cannot go to sleep.   10
Besides, in the sky the little birds fly,
And the hills are all covered with sheep.'

'Well, well go and play till the light fades away,
And then go home to bed.'
The little ones leaped and shouted and laughed   15
And all the hills echoèd.

'Infant Joy'

This poem again celebrates mother and child intimacy, although it may well be that the parent is already trying to manipulate her child's innocence by putting her words into the baby's mouth. This might be a rather harsh interpretation, however, and may run against the mood of the poem.

- How does the illustration on page 88 affect your understanding of the poem? The open flower may well seem like a nativity scene, but what of the drooping one?
- Coleridge, the Romantic poet and critic whose beliefs were in many ways similar to Blake's own, objected that a two-day-old infant cannot in fact speak. Does this matter to you?

✦ *Activity*

Present a collage of mother–child images, with the poem as the central focus.

Infant Joy

'I have no name;
I am but two days old.'
What shall I call thee?
'I happy am;
Joy is my name.'   5
Sweet joy befall thee!

Pretty joy!
Sweet joy but two days old,
Sweet joy I call thee.
Thou dost smile;   10
I sing the while.
Sweet joy befall thee.

'A Dream'

Dreams clearly fascinated Blake, and in this one anxiety is replaced by comfort and security.

- What might the emmet (l. 3 – an ant) and glow-worm (l. 14) symbolise?
- Does the dream setting of the poem suggest that such a sense of security is unlikely to be found in the cold light of day?

✦ *Activity*

Consider whether dreams have a wider significance. Research Sigmund Freud's ideas on the language of dreams. Imagine and script a psychiatrist explaining to the 'patient' this particular dream's meaning.

A Dream

Once a dream did weave a shade
  O'er my angel-guarded bed,
  That an emmet lost its way
Where on grass methought I lay.

Troubled, wildered and forlorn,   5
  Dark, benighted, travel-worn,
  Over many a tangled spray
All heart-broke I heard her say:

'Oh my children! Do they cry?
  Do they hear their father sigh?   10
  Now they look abroad to see,
Now return and weep for me.'

  Pitying I dropped a tear;
  But I saw a glow-worm near,
Who replied: 'What wailing wight   15
Calls the watchman of the night?

  'I am set to light the ground,
While the beetle goes his round.
  Follow now the beetle's hum.
Little wanderer hie thee home.'   20

'On Another's Sorrow'

As in several of the 'Songs of Innocence', anxiety again gives way to security, although the form of this poem, as a series of questions, perhaps implies doubt as to whether this sense of harmony is indeed always the case.

- What is your interpretation of the double denial in the third stanza?
- Several of the images of the poem could well relate to previous 'Songs'. Aim to fit poems to the various images presented.
- What do you understand by compassion as portrayed here? Does another person sharing one's own grief somehow lessen it? Is compassion always painful? Who represents compassion in this poem?

✦ *Activities and approaches*

1 Choose a quotation from the poem as a subtitle for your own short story or piece of descriptive writing.

2 In pairs, devise a dialogue between a Samaritan and a person in some sort of desperate plight, to bring out the meaning of the poem. You could use the poem or part of it in this presentation.

On Another's Sorrow

Can I see another's woe,
And not be in sorrow too?
Can I see another's grief
And not seek for kind relief?

Can I see a falling tear,   5
And not feel my sorrow's share?
Can a father see his child
Weep, nor be with sorrow filled?

Can a mother sit, and hear
An infant groan, an infant fear? 10
No, no, never can it be.
Never, never can it be.

And can he who smiles on all
Hear the wren with sorrows small,
Hear the small bird's grief and care, 15
Hear the woes that infants bear –

And not sit beside the nest,
Pouring pity in their breast;
And not sit the cradle near
Weeping tear on infant's tear; 20

And not sit both night and day,
Wiping all our tears away?
Oh no! never can it be.
Never, never can it be.

He doth give his joy to all. 25
He becomes an infant small.
He becomes a man of woe.
He doth feel the sorrow too.

Think not thou canst sigh a sigh,
And thy maker is not by. 30
Think not thou canst weep a tear,
And thy maker is not near.

Oh! he gives to us his joy,
That our grief he may destroy,
Till our grief is fled and gone 35
He doth sit by us and moan.

'Introduction' to 'Songs of Experience' and 'Earth's Answer'

This is a far more complex introduction than that to the 'Songs of Innocence', reflecting the problematic nature of Blake's relationship with the state of experience. The bard is a favourite figure of the Romantic movement, combining art with prophecy, and here he has insight into a damaging conflict between the 'lapsèd soul' of man and the female figure of 'Earth', who in the second part of this pair of poems gives her forlorn answer.

- In the sense that both this pair of poems and the 'Introduction' to 'Innocence' present dialogues, is there any common ground? Any contrast?
- What is the significance of 'The Holy Word' (l. 4)?
- Why has the soul lapsed? Is this the meaning of experience?
- Who exactly is 'Calling the lapsèd soul' (l. 6): the bard, or the Holy Word? Does it matter?
- What is being demanded of Earth here?
- Why is Earth female, and the Holy Word or lapsed soul apparently male?
- Are 'The starry floor' and 'The wat'ry shore' (ll. 18–19) images of beauty or desolation? Does it depend on who is speaking?
- Does 'tillthe break of day' (l. 20) suggest a long or short time spell?
- Explain in your own words the gist of Earth's answer (p. 47).
- What happens to the rhyme scheme in 'Earth's Answer'? What may be the significance here?

Introduction

Hear the voice of the bard!
Who present, past, and future sees;
Whose ears have heard
The Holy Word,
That walked among the ancient trees   5

Calling the lapsèd soul,
And weeping in the evening dew;
That might control
The starry pole,
And fallen, fallen light renew!   10

'O Earth, O Earth return!
Arise from out the dewy grass.
Night is worn,
And the morn
Rises from the slumberous mass.   15

'Turn away no more;
Why wilt thou turn away?
The starry floor,
The wat'ry shore,
Is giv'n thee till the break of day.'   20

✦ *Activities and approaches*

1 Blake wrote elsewhere about the nature of prophecy:

> Every honest man is a Prophet; he utters his opinion on private
> & public matters. Thus: If you go on So, the result is So. He
> never says, such a thing shall happen let you do so what you
> will. A Prophet is a Seer, not an Arbitrary Dictator.
>
> (from Blake's marginal notes to Watson's
> 'An Apology for the Bible')

Consider how these views relate to the bard's warning to Earth,
or, more generally, to Blake's view of himself as a prophet.

2 'Storyboard' the poem as a series of stills for a short film entitled
Battle of the Sexes. Concentrate on the communication or lack
of it between the main characters – a contrast to the intuitive
understanding so frequently found between Blake's innocent
characters and symbols.

3 List all the words you can find associated with joy and with
misery. Read the poems aloud in choral style, echoing first the
'joy' words, then the 'misery' words. Which is the dominant
mood, do you think?

4 Imagine and write a play script in which both male and female
characters seek advice about their problems as represented in
these poems from a neutral well-wisher – perhaps one of the
characters from 'Innocence' who seems so adept at solving
predicaments.

Earth's Answer

Earth raised up her head
From the darkness dread and drear.
Her light fled –
Stony dread! –
And her locks covered with grey despair.   5

'Prisoned on wat'ry shore
Starry jealousy does keep my den.
Cold and hoar,
Weeping o'er,
I hear the father of the ancient men.   10

'Selfish father of men
Cruel, jealous, selfish fear!
Can delight
Chained in night
The virgins of youth and morning bear?   15

'Does spring hide its joy
When buds and blossoms grow?
Does the sower
Sow by night?
Or the ploughman in darkness plough?   20

'Break this heavy chain
That does freeze my bones around.
Selfish! Vain!
Eternal bane!
That free love with bondage bound.'   25

'The Clod and the Pebble'

In this poem innocence and experience exist side by side: the difficulty is in deciding which comes out more attractively.

- What does the nature of both clods of clay and pebbles as physical entities tell you about their use in the poem as symbols of human attitudes?
- In Blake's 'The Book of Thel' (1789) a clod of clay attains salvation despite being merely a 'meanest thing'. Is this a clue to understanding 'The Clod and the Pebble', or has Blake's thought moved on since writing that poem?
- What irony do you find here in relation to either symbol?
- Is there any common ground between the clod and the pebble? Which comes out more attractively? More realistically?

✦ *Activities and approaches*

1 Try to match the clod and the pebble to other characters and symbols in *Songs of Innocence and of Experience*. Do you learn anything from this matching exercise about how the clod and pebble might act in different situations?

2 Assign clod- and pebble-like qualities to two or more invented characters of your own and then explore their attitudes and relationships in a short dramatic presentation.

The Clod and the Pebble

'Love seeketh not itself to please,
Nor for itself hath any care,
But for another gives its ease,
And builds a Heaven in Hell's despair.'

So sang a little Clod of Clay,   5
Trodden with the cattle's feet,
But a Pebble of the brook
Warbled out these metres meet:

'Love seeketh only self to please,
To bind another to its delight,   10
Joys in another's loss of ease,
And builds a Hell in Heaven's despite.'

'Holy Thursday'

Here is a direct contrast to the identically titled poem in 'Innocence', and also a contrast to various other 'Songs', referring to the same event as previously but seen with completely different eyes.

- Where else is there a series of questions? Are they similar? What may be the intended answers, if any, to the questions?
- How is it possible for the same place to be 'a rich and fruitful land' (l. 2) and 'a land of poverty' (l. 8)? Can this apparent paradox be applied to today's world?
- Why is the feeding hand 'usurous' (l. 4)?
- How does the style of the poem, with each line end-stopped, aid your interpretation?
- What irony is there here, particularly in the last stanza?

✦ *Activities and approaches*

1 Write a reasoned critique and a defence of the practice of charity, using evidence from the poem to back up your arguments.

2 Imagine you are one of the beadles, more used to the generous view of your role in the 'Innocence' poem, and write a letter complaining of misrepresentation to the 'Experience' observer.

3 Use the poem as the centrepiece of a collage which presents images of wealth and poverty today.

Holy Thursday

Is this a holy thing to see,
In a rich and fruitful land:
Babes reduced to misery,
Fed with cold and usurous hand?

Is that trembling cry a song?   5
Can it be a song of joy?
And so many children poor?
It is a land of poverty!

And their sun does never shine,
And their fields are bleak and bare,   10
And their ways are filled with thorns;
It is eternal winter there.

For where'er the sun does shine,
And where'er the rain does fall –
Babe can never hunger there,   15
Nor poverty the mind appal.

'The Little Girl Lost' and 'The Little Girl Found'

Originally in the 'Songs of Innocence' but later transferred by Blake to 'Experience', this pair of relatively long poems may suggest fairy-tale or mythical events.

- Describe the various elements of the illustrations on pages 89 and 90. How does each image play its part in helping your understanding of the poem?
- Describe what is happening in these poems. What might be represented by the events described?
- The wild desert blooming (ll. 7–8) has Biblical significance. Research Isaiah 35:1, and the Greek myth of Persephone and Demeter, which has direct relevance.
- Are these poems, particularly the opening and closing pairs of stanzas, optimistic or pessimistic in tone? Do you think they are better placed in 'Innocence' or 'Experience'?

✦ *Activities and approaches*

1 Present a dramatised or mimed version of the poems, or try using dance and music to express the emotions and events.

2 Parents and daughter give their versions of the events: role-play these presentations.

The Little Girl Lost

In futurity
I prophetic see
That the earth from sleep
(Grave the sentence deep)

Shall arise and seek   5
For her maker meek,
And the desert wild
Become a garden mild.

In the southern clime,
Where the summer's prime   10
Never fades away,
Lovely Lyca lay.

Seven summers old
Lovely Lyca told;
She had wandered long,   15
Hearing wild birds' song.

'Sweet sleep come to me
Underneath this tree;
Do father, mother weep?
Where can Lyca sleep?   20

'Lost in desert wild
Is your little child.
How can Lyca sleep,
If her mother weep?

'If her heart does ache,   25
Then let Lyca wake;
If my mother sleep,
Lyca shall not weep.

'Frowning, frowning night,
O'er this desert bright,   30
Let thy moon arise
While I close my eyes.'

Sleeping Lyca lay,
While the beasts of prey,
Come from caverns deep,   35
Viewed the maid asleep.

The kingly lion stood
And the virgin viewed,
Then he gambolled round
O'er the hallowed ground.   40

Leopards, tigers play
Round her as she lay,
While the lion old
Bowed his mane of gold,

And her bosom lick,   45
And upon her neck;
From his eyes of flame
Ruby tears there came;

While the lioness
Loosed her slender dress   50
And naked they conveyed
To caves the sleeping maid.

The Little Girl Found

All the night in woe
Lyca's parents go,
Over valleys deep
While the deserts weep.

Tired and woe-begone,   5
Hoarse with making moan,
Arm in arm seven days
They traced the desert ways.

Seven nights they sleep
Among shadows deep,   10
And dream they see their child
Starved in desert wild.

Pale through pathless ways
The fancied image strays,
Famished, weeping, weak,   15
With hollow piteous shriek.

Rising from unrest,
The trembling woman pressed
With feet of weary woe;
She could no further go.   20

In his arms he bore
Her, armed with sorrow sore,
Till before their way
A couching lion lay.

Turning back was vain.   25
Soon his heavy mane
Bore them to the ground;
Then he stalked around,

Smelling his prey;
But their fears allay 30
When he licks their hands,
And silent by them stands.

They look upon his eyes,
Filled with deep surprise,
And wondering behold 35
A spirit armed in gold.

On his head a crown,
On his shoulders down
Flowed his golden hair.
Gone was all their care. 40

'Follow me,' he said,
'Weep not for the maid;
In my palace deep,
Lyca lies asleep.'

Then they followèd 45
Where the vision led,
And saw their sleeping child,
Among tigers wild.

To this day they dwell
In a lonely dell, 50
Nor fear the wolvish howl,
Nor the lion's growl.

'The Tiger'

One of Blake's most famous poems, 'The Tiger' has been interpreted in many different – sometimes opposing – ways. As a
contrast to 'The Lamb' of 'Innocence', the tiger clearly has ag-
gressive and fiercely energetic qualities – and yet there is much to
admire in this fierce energy.

- Compare the first draft (p. 58) to the finished poem (p. 59).
  What differences are there in effect? Is the final version better?
- How does the rhythm, with the frequently stressed first syllable
  of the words, accentuate the power and energy of the tiger?
- List the images of fire, light and darkness. How is the presence
  of the creature heightened by these images?
- Who is asking the questions? What is the central question?
- What evidence is there of creativity, which Blake intensely
  admired, in the poem? Of destructiveness?
- Is the 'smile' (l. 19) sinister or joyful?
- Compare the text with the illustration on page 94. Do they
  complement or contradict each other? Describe the tiger's
  appearance.
- Why does 'Could' (l. 4) become 'Dare' (l. 24)?
- What do you understand by 'frame thy fearful symmetry'
  (l. 24)?
- What questions would you like to ask Blake about this poem?
  What do you think his answers might be?

✦ *Activities and approaches*

1 Much of the poem is in the form of a series of questions, a
  familiar pattern in Blake's poetry. Imagine and write the creator's – whoever that is – response to these questions.

2 Use the poem as a focus for a conservation poster on the tiger's
  plight in the modern world.

The Tiger
(first draft)

Tiger, Tiger, burning bright
In the forests of the night,
What immortal hand or eye
Dare frame thy fearful symmetry?

Burnt in distant deeps or skies   5
The cruel fire of thine eyes?
On what wings dare he aspire?
What the hand dare sieze the fire?

And what shoulder and what art
Could twist the sinews of thy heart?   10
And when thy heart began to beat
What dread hand and what dread feet

Could fetch it from the furnace deep
And in thy horrid ribs dare steep
In the well of sanguine woe?   15
In what clay and in what mould
Were thy eyes of fury roll'd?

Where the hammer? Where the chain?
In what furnace was thy brain?
What the anvil? What dread grasp   20
Dare its deadly terrors clasp?

When the stars threw down their spears
And water'd heaven with their tears
Dare he laugh his work to see?
Dare he who made the lamb make thee?   25

Tiger, Tiger, burning bright
In the forests of the night,
What immortal hand and eye
Dare frame thy fearful symmetry?

The Tiger

Tiger, tiger, burning bright,
In the forests of the night:
What immortal hand or eye
Could frame thy fearful symmetry?

In what distant deeps or skies,　　　　5
Burnt the fire of thine eyes?
On what wings dare he aspire?
What the hand dare seize the fire?

And what shoulder, and what art,
Could twist the sinews of thy heart?　　10
And when thy heart began to beat,
What dread hand? and what dread feet?

What the hammer? what the chain?
In what furnace was thy brain?
What the anvil? what dread grasp　　15
Dare its deadly terrors clasp?

When the stars threw down their spears,
And watered Heaven with their tears,
Did he smile his work to see?
Did he who made the lamb make thee?　　20

Tiger, tiger, burning bright,
In the forests of the night:
What immortal hand or eye
Dare frame thy fearful symmetry?

'The Chimney-Sweeper'

Like the 'Innocence' poem of the same title, this is a response to the plight of boys and girls forced to climb up blackened narrow chimneys to sweep them.

- How significant is it that the parents have gone to church (l. 4)?
- What does 'Because' (l. 5) suggest about parental attitudes towards the innocence celebrated in so many of Blake's poems?
- What do you make of Blake's attitude towards Church and state?
- How is 'heaven' linked to 'misery' (l. 12), usually opposite?
- The original line 12 was 'who wrap themselves up in our misery'. Which is the more effective?
- How does the illustration on page 92 emphasise the poem's impact?

✦ *Activities and approaches*

1 Play the roles of the father and mother facing hostile audience questions in a 'hot-seating' exercise.

2 Write out the words of the prayer uttered by the parents.

3 Imagine the 'Innocence' poem to be the youthful thoughts of the now older, cynical 'Experience' sweep. Script the conversation between the latter and a young, frightened 'recruit'.

The Chimney-Sweeper

A little black thing among the snow,
Crying 'weep, weep' in notes of woe!
'Where are thy father and mother? Say!'
'They are both gone up to the church to pray.

'Because I was happy upon the heath,   5
And smiled among the winter's snow,
They clothed me in the clothes of death,
And taught me to sing the notes of woe.

'And because I am happy and dance and sing,
They think they have done me no injury,   10
And are gone to praise God and his priest and king,
Who make up a heaven of our misery.'

'Nurse's Song'

Another directly contrasting poem to that of 'Innocence'; here the nurse seems embittered and jealous of the children's pleasure. The setting seems the same, but the view is entirely different.

- Why do you think this nurse looks back on her own childhood with such horror?
- Why is there only one narrator in the poem, compared to the 'Innocence' version?
- What has happened to the location of innocence here?
- Why is 'disguise' (l. 8) mentioned?

✦ Activities and approaches

1 Script a dialogue between the innocent and experienced practitioners in a college for the training of children's nurses.

2 The child, now some years later as an adult, reminisces about two very different nurses. Give his or her thoughts in the form of a monologue.

'The Sick Rose'

Often taken in conjunction with and contrast to 'The Blossom'.

- How does the illustration on page 93 affect your interpretation of the poem? Compare with 'The Blossom' on page 85.
- What qualities of a rose make it a particularly apt symbol here? What of the worm?
- What are the key words of this poem? Construct a cluster diagram of these words with appropriate associations for each.

✦ Activities and approaches

1 Imagine and script the reply of the rose to the poet, considering who you think the speaker is in the poem.

2 Anthologise images of the rose from various sources, including other poems such as those by W. B. Yeats, for example 'To the Rose Upon the Rood of Time' and 'The Secret Rose'. How do these images help your understanding of Blake's poem?

Nurse's Song

When the voices of children are heard on the green,
  And whisperings are in the dale,
The days of my youth rise fresh in my mind,
  My face turns green and pale.

Then come home my children, the sun is gone down,   5
  And the dews of night arise.
Your spring and your day are wasted in play,
  And your winter and night in disguise.

The Sick Rose

O rose, thou art sick;
The invisible worm
That flies in the night,
In the howling storm,

Has found out thy bed   5
Of crimson joy,
And his dark secret love
Does thy life destroy.

'The Fly'

This is a short and direct poem, perhaps reflecting the often momentary guilt we all may feel on needlessly taking a fellow creature's life.

- What might the speaker's motives be for writing this poem?
- How do the rhythm and diction of the poem relate to the subject matter?
- Comment on the irony of the poem.
- King Lear in Shakespeare's play of that name reflects on mankind's unhappy lot on this earth:

  As flies to wanton boys are we to the Gods;
  They kill us for their sport.

  What is the symbolic role of Blake's fly?
- Why, in view of the apparently happy and carefree conclusion to the poem, is it included in 'Experience'?

✦ *Activity*
Imagine and script the fly's reply to the speaker.

The Fly

Little fly,
Thy summer's play
My thoughtless hand
Has brushed away.

Am not I   5
A fly like thee?
Or art not thou
A man like me?

For I dance
And drink and sing,   10
Till some blind hand
Shall brush my wing.

If thought is life
And strength and breath,
And the want   15
Of thought is death,

Then am I
A happy fly,
If I live,
Or if I die.   20

'The Angel'

This dream poem has distinctly nightmarish qualities and a rather desolate conclusion, contrasting strongly with the dreams of 'Innocence'.

- What does this poem suggest about love and innocence?
- What do you understand by line 4, a 'difficult' line?
- Is it important that the dreamer is female?
- Who or what do you think the angel might represent?
- Why do you think 'the morn blushed rosy red' (l. 10)? Is this an image of beauty, shame or corruption?
- In what sense are fears armed?
- Might this poem have a contrary 'Song of Innocence'? Which one, if any?

✦ *Activities and approaches*

1 Use the ideas in the poem to imagine a psychiatrist's session with a patient. Script the dialogue that might occur.

2 Imagine what sort of picture would best accompany the poem. Look at some art books for ideas to enhance the meaning.

The Angel

I dreamt a dream! – What can it mean! –
And that I was a maiden queen,
Guarded by an angel mild.
Witless woe was ne'er beguiled!

And I wept both night and day, 5
And he wiped my tears away,
And I wept both day and night,
And hid from him my heart's delight.

So he took his wings and fled;
Then the morn blushed rosy red. 10
I dried my tears, and armed my fear
With ten thousand shields and spears.

Soon my angel came again.
I was armed; he came in vain,
For the time of youth was fled, 15
And grey hairs were on my head.

'My Pretty Rose Tree'

This poem is sometimes regarded as autobiographical, dealing with Blake's marriage and the temptations outside it. It is misleading to assume the narrator's voice is Blake's own, however.

- How does the flower imagery assist your understanding?
- Does 'only' (l. 8) imply something unique and special, or simply meagre? In any case, how can thorns provide 'delight'?

✦ Activity
Use a quotation from the poem as a subtitle for writing a short story on the theme of jealousy.

'Ah! Sunflower'

This is a poem of yearning, which is never apparently resolved.

- Why does the exclamatory 'Ah!' appear in the title?
- What do you see in the contrast between 'golden' and 'pale'?
- Who is the 'traveller' and what is the 'journey' (l. 4)?
- Is the sunflower's desire ultimately fulfilled or not? Consider the absence of any main verb in this context.

✦ Activity
In a small group, dramatise the poem and then organise a series of 'tableaux' to present the meaning of the poem.

'The Lily'

The lily suggests, traditionally, innocence.

- In view of this association, why is the poem in 'Experience'?
- How does the lily fit with the other flowers of the trio?
- What qualities are symbolised by the lily?

✦ Activity
Assemble a collage of flower paintings and photographs to include rose, sunflower and lily. Suggest in the design the relationship between these flowers.

My Pretty Rose Tree

A flower was offered to me,
Such a flower as May never bore,
But I said, 'I've a pretty rose tree,'
And I passed the sweet flower o'er.

Then I went to my pretty rose tree,   5
To tend her by day and by night,
But my rose turned away with jealousy,
And her thorns were my only delight.

Ah! Sunflower

Ah! sunflower, weary of time,
Who countest the steps of the sun,
Seeking after that sweet golden clime
Where the traveller's journey is done;

Where the youth pined away with desire,   5
And the pale virgin shrouded in snow,
Arise from their graves and aspire;
Where my sunflower wishes to go.

The Lily

The modest rose puts forth a thorn,
The humble sheep a threat'ning horn;
While the lily white shall in love delight,
Nor a thorn nor a threat stain her beauty bright.

'The Garden of Love'

This poem appears to continue the horticultural imagery, and contrasts directly with the 'Echoing Green' of 'Innocence'. Here the dead weight of repression has replaced the freedom of expression so evident in the earlier poem.

- What does the phrase 'Thou shalt not' (l. 6) imply about Blake's views on the established Church?
- What associations, pleasant or otherwise, does the garden convey? How does a garden compare with a green?
- What do you think are the 'joys and desires' (l. 12)?
- Do the 'briars' (l. 12) suggest a particular association? If so, how is the meaning of this and possibly other poems enhanced?

✦ *Activities and approaches*

1 Imagine and write a different story about an adult returning to a favourite childhood haunt to find it destructively changed.

2 Write the priest's sermon to parishoners defending the new regime which has replaced the garden of love.

'The Little Vagabond'

This poem appears to advocate the use of alcohol as part of Christian worship. Many in the nineteenth century were prepared to accept beer drinking as a harmless, convivial pursuit, in contrast to the destructive use of cheap, rough gin. Look at some of Hogarth's prints, notably 'Gin Lane' and a companion print 'Beer Street' celebrating the virtues of beer drinking. Interestingly, this poem was left out of the first published editions of *Songs of Innocence and of Experience* after Blake's death.

- Who do you think 'modest dame Lurch' (l. 11) is? Is her modesty a virtue here?
- The last stanza links alcohol with more general themes. What do you think the little vagabond is meaning here?

✦ *Activity*

Imagine and write the mother's reply to the little vagabond's plea.

The Garden of Love

I went to the Garden of Love,
And saw what I never had seen:
A chapel was built in the midst,
Where I used to play on the green.

And the gates of this chapel were shut, 5
And 'Thou shalt not' writ over the door;
So I turned to the Garden of Love,
That so many sweet flowers bore.

And I saw it was filled with graves,
And tomb-stones where flowers should be, 10
And priests in black gowns were walking their rounds,
And binding with briars my joys and desires.

The Little Vagabond

Dear mother, dear mother, the church is cold,
But the ale-house is healthy and pleasant and warm.
Besides, I can tell where I am used well;
Such usage in Heaven will never do well.

But if at the church they would give us some ale, 5
And a pleasant fire our souls to regale,
We'd sing and we'd pray all the live-long day,
Nor ever once wish from the church to stray.

Then the parson might preach and drink and sing,
And we'd be as happy as birds in the spring; 10
And modest dame Lurch, who is always at church,
Would not have bandy children, nor fasting, nor birch.

And God, like a father rejoicing to see
His children as pleasant and happy as he,
Would have no more quarrel with the Devil or the barrel, 15
But kiss him and give him both drink and apparel.

'London'

This poem seems to deal with a sense of urban alienation. Yet Blake lived nearly all his life in London and thrived on the city life. London became his potentially ideal city of Jerusalem.

- Note that in early drafts of the poem, Blake wrote 'dirty' instead of 'chartered' (ll. 1 and 2), and had a different final stanza:

> But most the midnight harlot's curse
> From every dismal street I hear,
> Weaves around the marriage hearse
> And blasts the new born infant's tear.

Why did Blake make the changes? Explore especially the meaning of 'chartered'.

- Study page 95. Does it help your understanding of the poem?
- 'mark' (ll. 3 and 4) may mean 'notice' and 'remark', or a physical mark. Which fits better here?
- 'ban' (l. 7) means 'swear word'. Are there other meanings?
- Which senses are appealed to in the poem, and how?
- In what sense are the manacles 'mind-forged' (l. 8)?
- New churches quickly turned black in the polluted atmosphere of London. What else may 'black'ning' (l. 10) imply?
- 'appalls' (l. 10) suggests 'filling with dread', but refers also to the dark cloth used at funerals. How appropriate is this?
- 'plagues' (l. 16) are sexually transmitted disease, known to affect victims' babies. What symbolic meaning is there also?
- Are there any signs of hope in this poem?
- What are the links between sweep and church (check previous poems), soldier and palace, and harlot and marriage?

✦ *Activities and approaches*

1 Imagine the stories of the sweep, the soldier and the harlot, then present them as 'talking heads' to the wider audience.

2 The poem is engraved on the pavement of the Thames embankment. Use it as a focus for images of the city by creating a collage of pictures and words.

London

I wander through each chartered street,
Near where the chartered Thames does flow,
And mark in every face I meet
Marks of weakness, marks of woe.

In every cry of every man, 5
In every infant's cry of fear,
In every voice, in every ban,
The mind-forged manacles I hear:

How the chimney-sweeper's cry
Every black'ning church appalls, 10
And the hapless soldier's sigh
Runs in blood down palace walls.

But most through midnight streets I hear
How the youthful harlot's curse
Blasts the new-born infant's tear, 15
And blights with plagues the marriage hearse.

'The Human Abstract'

Here is opposition to 'The Divine Image' of 'Innocence', and the negative aspect of human nature is vividly expressed. Interestingly, though, Blake's first title for the poem was a repetition of the 'image' idea – 'The Human Image'. The first draft makes illuminating comparative reading, as it included six final extra lines:

> They said this mystery never shall cease;
> The priest promotes war and the soldier peace.
>
> There souls of men are bought and sold,
> And milk-fed infancy for gold;
> And youth to slaughter houses led,
> And beauty for a bit of bread.

- Who is speaking? Is there a change in speaker after the first stanza? Any further changes?
- How does the mention of 'Pity' (l. 1) compare with Blake's presentation of this emotion elsewhere?
- How does humility come into the picture? Compare with other explorations of humility by Blake.
- How does the illustration on page 96 affect your understanding?
- Study the imagery of creatures and of darkness. What is implied?
- Why is the 'fruit of Deceit' (l. 17) so attractive? Does this quality reflect other myths, Bible stories or fairy-tales?
- Make a detailed comparison with the longer first draft. Which is the more effective?

✦ *Activities and approaches*

1 'Mutual fear brings peace' (l. 5). Write a justification of the retention of nuclear weapons under this title, and an opposing tract.

2 Imagine and draw the tree depicted in the poem.

The Human Abstract ·

Pity would be no more
If we did not make somebody poor,
And Mercy no more could be
If all were as happy as we.

And mutual fear brings Peace,   5
Till the selfish loves increase.
Then Cruelty knits a snare,
And spreads his baits with care.

He sits down with holy fears,
And waters the ground with tears;   10
Then Humility takes its root
Underneath his foot.

Soon spreads the dismal shade
Of Mystery over his head,
And the caterpillar and fly   15
Feed on the Mystery.

And it bears the fruit of Deceit,
Ruddy and sweet to eat,
And the raven his nest has made
In its thickest shade.   20

The gods of the earth and sea
Sought through Nature to find this tree,
But their search was all in vain.
There grows one in the human brain.

'Infant Sorrow'

This is the contrasting poem to 'Infant Joy': the energy of infancy is quickly threatened.

- Do you think infants have conscious thoughts and strategies like this? How would we know? Is an adult assigning his or her cynical motives to the infant in this poem?
- Look at 'piping' (l. 3) in other poems? Is there any similarity?
- Are 'swaddling bands' (l. 6) necessary restraints in this context?
- What sounds greet the infant? What do they say of the world?
- Why do you think the baby is 'Like a fiend hid in a cloud' (l. 4)?
- What differences are there in the baby's attitude to father and mother? Is the child male or female? Does it matter?

✦ Activities and approaches

1 Imagine and write a playscript of parents discussing the behaviour of their 'difficult' child.

2 Present a dramatised contrast, perhaps as a pair of tableaux, between the children of 'Infant Joy' and those in 'Infant Sorrow'.

'A Poison Tree'

This poem comments on the destructive nature of repressed feelings; as so often, Blake seems to prefigure psychoanalysis.

- Compare the apple to that of 'The Human Abstract'. What is the significance, in Blake's poems and elsewhere, of the fruit, the garden, the tree and night?
- Is it significant that 'he knew that it was mine' (l. 12)?
- Why did Blake originally entitle the poem 'Christian Forbearance'? Which title do you prefer?
- 'pole' (l. 14) means 'the sky'. Is the veiling significant here?

✦ Activities and approaches

1 Imagine and mime a possible story illustrating the poem.

2 Use tableaux to present the key moments in the narrative.

3 Imagine and write the foe's dying thoughts.

Infant Sorrow

My mother groaned, my father wept!
Into the dangerous world I leapt,
Helpless, naked, piping loud,
Like a fiend hid in a cloud.

Struggling in my father's hands,   5
Striving against my swaddling bands,
Bound and weary, I thought best
To sulk upon my mother's breast.

A Poison Tree

I was angry with my friend;
I told my wrath – my wrath did end.
I was angry with my foe;
I told it not – my wrath did grow.

And I watered it in fears,   5
Night and morning with my tears,
And I sunnèd it with smiles,
And with soft deceitful wiles.

And it grew both day and night,
Till it bore an apple bright.   10
And my foe beheld it shine,
And he knew that it was mine,

And into my garden stole
When the night had veiled the pole.
In the morning glad I see   15
My foe outstretched beneath the tree.

'A Little Boy Lost'

Directly opposing 'The Little Boy Lost' of 'Innocence', this poem ends in misery rather than harmonious resolution. The boy's statement of his love for his father in the first two stanzas could be seen as deliberately provocative or as a bald statement of the truth of human nature: explore Cordelia's response to her father at the start of Shakespeare's *King Lear* for an apt comparison. However we take it, the priest in the poem reacts violently and the grieving parents are unwilling or unable to intervene in this drastic punishment.

- What essentially is the priest's argument against the boy?
- How does the word 'little' (ll. 11 and 19) affect your reactions?
- Explore Blake's views on 'Mystery' here and elsewhere. Is there attraction in the mysterious?
- As so often, a question is posed: what is the intended response? 'Albion' (l. 24) signifies England.
- Why do you think the subject of the poem is male?

✦ *Activity*

Imagine and write a play script of the court case that would arise concerning child abuse when the boy, saved from almost certain death by burning, makes a complaint at his treatment. We should hear from the parents, priest, boy, and defence and prosecution lawyers.

A Little Boy Lost

'Nought loves another as itself,
   Nor venerates another so,
   Nor is it possible to thought
A greater than itself to know.

'And father, how can I love you,   5
   Or any of my brothers more?
   I love you like the little bird
That picks up crumbs around the door.'

The priest sat by and heard the child;
   In trembling zeal he seized his hair.   10
   He led him by his little coat,
And all admired the priestly care.

And, standing on the altar high,
   'Lo, what a fiend is here!' said he,
   'One who sets reason up for judge   15
   Of our most holy mystery.'

The weeping child could not be heard;
   The weeping parents wept in vain.
   They stripped him to his little shirt,
And bound him in an iron chain,   20

And burned him in a holy place,
   Where many had been burned before.
   The weeping parents wept in vain.
Are such things done on Albion's shore?

'A Little Girl Lost'

The poem contrasts with the 'Innocence' version, and the quatrain of righteous indignation (ll. 1–4) underlines Blake's claim to prophecy, in the sense of giving warnings to the human race. Clearly, love is celebrated here, as in the 'Innocence' poem, but there is now no peaceful conclusion. We sense with compassion the pain of the father as clearly as that of the maiden Ona, whose love is unfulfilled. Blake was influenced by early feminist thinkers like Mary Wollstonecraft, whom he knew personally and deeply admired, in his conception of female sexuality.

- Why do this poem and 'A Little Boy Lost' have 'a' in the title, rather than 'the' as in other 'Songs of Experience'?
- Why is the father's 'loving look' likened to 'the holy book' (ll. 27–8)? Are there any echoes of other poems?
- What other stories are there of parental disapproval of love matches? Do they add further dimensions to this poem's meaning? Look in particular at Shakespeare's plays.
- What contradiction is there within the last line, with images of 'blossoms' and 'hoary [frosty] hair' (l. 34)?
- Is it significant that the maiden deals with her father? Would things have been different with her mother? Why is the 'father white' (l. 25)?
- Look at the rhyme scheme of the poem. What do you learn?
- To whom is the poem explicitly addressed? Does this matter?

✦ Activities and approaches

1 Imagine that the lovers manage to elope, and their story is taken up by a newspaper. Present this story, and include an interview with the father.

2 Arrange a choral reading of the poem, contrasting the words of enlightenment with the words of grief through the use of echoes.

A Little Girl Lost

Children of the future age,
Reading this indignant page,
Know that in a former time
Love! sweet love! was thought a crime.

    In the age of gold,   5
Free from winter's cold,
Youth and maiden bright,
To the holy light,
Naked in the sunny beams delight.

    Once a youthful pair,   10
Filled with softest care,
Met in garden bright,
Where the holy light
Had just removed the curtains of the night.

    There in rising day   15
On the grass they play.
Parents were afar;
Strangers came not near;
And the maiden soon forgot her fear.

    Tired with kisses sweet,   20
They agree to meet
When the silent sleep
Waves o'er heavens deep,
And the weary, tired wanderers weep.

    To her father white   25
Came the maiden bright;
But his loving look,
Like the holy book,
All her tender limbs with terror shook.

    'Ona! pale and weak!   30
To thy father speak.
Oh the trembling fear!
Oh the dismal care,
That shakes the blossoms of my hoary hair!'

'The Schoolboy'

This poem was originally part of the 'Songs of Innocence' but was placed by Blake in 'Experience' for later editions. Certainly, the carefree innocence of the schoolboy is cruelly restricted, with the speaker's views clearly stated through a series of indignant questions couched in terms of a range of natural images.

- List the images of joy and freedom, and contrast with a similar list of images of repression. Which words suggest the dominant tone of the poem? Try to echo the specific words while reading aloud to decide this question.
- Is the poem better placed in 'Innocence' or 'Experience'?
- Does the schoolboy complain too much? After all, the sweep and little black boy in 'Innocence' have to put up with a great deal more.

✦ *Activities and approaches*

1 Imagine the head of the school in question hearing of the schoolboy's complaint, and script the defence he or she might make of institutional education.

2 Discuss how far your education might be seen as a means towards freedom, knowledge and enlightenment, or as a matter of social conditioning, repression and control.

The Schoolboy

I love to rise in a summer morn,
When the birds sing on every tree;
The distant huntsman winds his horn,
And the skylark sings with me.
Oh! what sweet company.   5

But to go to school in a summer morn,
Oh! it drives all joy away;
Under a cruel eye outworn,
The little ones spend the day
In sighing and dismay.   10

Ah! then at times I drooping sit,
And spend many an anxious hour,
Nor in my book can I take delight,
Nor sit in learning's bower,
Worn through with the dreary shower.   15

How can the bird that is born for joy
Sit in a cage and sing?
How can a child when fears annoy
But droop his tender wing,
And forget his youthful spring?   20

O father and mother! if buds are nipped,
And blossoms blown away,
And if the tender plants are stripped
Of their joy in the springing day,
By sorrow and care's dismay,   25

How shall the summer arise in joy,
Or the summer fruits appear?
Or how shall we gather what griefs destroy,
Or bless the mellowing year,
When the blasts of winter appear?   30

'The Voice of the Ancient Bard'

Some editions have placed this poem with 'Innocence' and other editions with 'Experience'.

- 'And wish to lead others when they should be led' (l. 11). How many of the characters of 'Experience' might this line apply to? Clearly, the fallen ones, stumbling and perplexed, suffer as well as those they inflict their restrictions upon.
- Who is the 'Ancient Bard' here? Is this Blake himself? How does the poem relate to the 'Introduction' to 'Songs of Experience'?

✦ *Activities*

1 Imagine and script the reply of one of the 'Experience' characters implicitly criticised in this poem in line 11.

2 The poem suggests an acute awareness of the problems of experience, but also, perhaps, a note of optimism. In the light of this, consider whether it is better placed in 'Innocence' or 'Experience'.

The Voice of the Ancient Bard

Youth of delight come hither
And see the opening morn,
Image of truth new-born.
Doubt is fled and clouds of reason,
Dark disputes and artful teasing.   5
Folly is an endless maze;
Tangled roots perplex her ways.
How many have fallen there!
They stumble all night over bones of the dead,
And feel they know not what but care,   10
And wish to lead others when they should be led.

84

'The Blossom' from *Songs of Innocence and of Experience*

'The Little Boy Lost' from *Songs of Innocence and of Experience*

'The Little Boy Found' from *Songs of Innocence and of Experience*

'Infant Joy' from *Songs of Innocence and of Experience*

'The Little Girl Lost' from *Songs of Innocence and of Experience*

'The Little Girl Found' from *Songs of Innocence and of Experience*

Introduction to 'Songs of Experience'

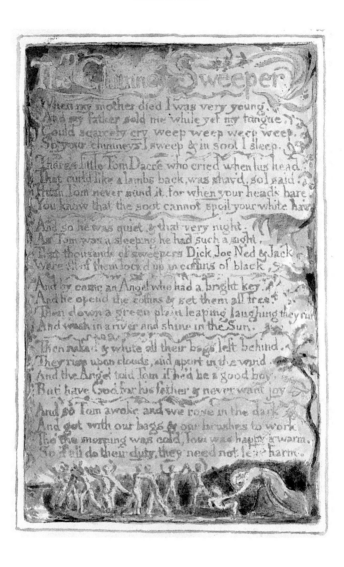

'The Chimney Sweeper' from *Songs of Innocence and of Experience*

'The Sick Rose' from *Songs of Innocence and of Experience*

'The Tyger' from *Songs of Innocence and of Experience*

'London' from *Songs of Innocence and of Experience*

'The Human Abstract' from *Songs of Innocence and of Experience*

'The Argument' from *The Marriage of Heaven and Hell*

Frontispiece to *The Marriage of Heaven and Hell*

Four Wood-Engravings for Thornton's *Virgil*

'Pity'

Extracts from *The Marriage of Heaven and Hell*

Blake probably began work on *The Marriage of Heaven and Hell* in 1789, and although it is likely that the book was finished in 1790, it was not presented as an illuminated manuscript until 1793. Blake's fascination with innocence and experience is evident from the nature of the 'Marriage': the title alone implies a desire to make apparent opposites come to terms with each other, although the actual relationship between innocence, experience, heaven and hell is a complex one. Blake was heavily influenced as a young man by Emmanuel Swedenborg, the mystical theologian who wrote, amongst other books, *Heaven and Hell* (1789). By the time Blake came to write the 'Marriage', however, he had turned away from the narrow moral stance of the Swedenborgian Church, and his attack on its philosophy has all the force of a disillusioned disciple.

◆ *Activities*

1 Study the title page illustration to *The Marriage of Heaven and Hell* on page 98. What is depicted? Does it prepare you for the content of the book?

2 What are the usual connotations of 'Heaven' and 'Hell'? Is it possible to talk of a reconciliation, or marriage, between them?

'The Argument'

Rintrah, a shadowy creation of Blake's imagination, presents an opening poem of furious wrath. As the poem progresses, we see the just man, in his rightful place, transforming the desert. However, the time of the just man is limited, as is the state of innocence, and the villain appears as if from nowhere to banish his adversary 'into barren climes'. Presumably, this is Blake himself: the prophet facing an age hostile to his words of warning, and we now see evil presenting a face of 'mild humility' while justice is left to profess wrathful indignation in the company of lions.

- Where else have you met the image of the desert blooming?
- What connection is there between the just man and the flowering of the desert?

- Is the 'vale of death' (l. 5) in fact the earthly life? Research Psalm 23 in the Bible for another dimension.
- Why is the villain characterised as a 'sneaking serpent' (l. 17)?
- Study the role of humility and wrath as presented in other writings by Blake. Do they amplify the meaning here?
- Is the anger felt by the just man justifiable? Is anger ever a positive emotion?

The prose section immediately following shows us even more closely Blake's claim to prophecy: he was thirty-three at the time of writing. Swedenborg is now seen as altogether too passive a figure to represent the just man in the age of the serpent. Blake develops his argument with Swedenborg forcefully throughout *The Marriage of Heaven and Hell* and the whole work can be read as a detailed critique of the Swedenborgian position.

Here, Blake summarises the conventional views on the nature and relationship of good and evil in order to demolish them. He deliberately and provocatively celebrates 'the active springing from energy', or, in the conventional terms of Blake's time, evil. 'The Argument', almost literally, is a warning of devil's advocacy.

- 'Without contraries is no progression'. What do you make of this assertion? Could this maxim be applied to everyday life? Could it, perhaps, be applied to innocence and experience in Blake's own presentation of these qualities?

The Argument

Rintrah roars and shakes his fires in the burden'd air;
Hungry clouds swag on the deep.

Once meek, and in a perilous path,
The just man kept his course along
The vale of death.   5
Roses are planted where thorns grow,
And on the barren heath
Sing the honey bees.

Then the perilous path was planted,
   And a river and a spring   10
   On every cliff and tomb,
  And on the bleached bones
   Red clay brought forth;

Till the villain left the paths of ease,
To walk in perilous paths, and drive   15
  The just man into barren climes.

Now the sneaking serpent walks
   In mild humility,
And the just man rages in the wilds
   Where lions roam.   20

Rintrah roars and shakes his fires in the burden'd air;
  Hungry clouds swag on the deep.

As a new Heaven is begun, and it is now thirty-three
years since its advent, the eternal Hell revives. And lo!
Swedenborg is the angel sitting at the tomb: his writ-   25
ings are the linen clothes folded up. Now is the domi-
nion of Edom, and the return of Adam into Paradise;
see Isaiah xxxiv and xxxv Chap.

   Without contraries is no progression. Attraction and
repulsion, reason and energy, love and hate, are   30
necessary to human existence.

   From these contraries spring what the religious call
good and evil. Good is the passive that obeys reason.
Evil is the active springing from energy.

   Good is Heaven. Evil is Hell.   35

'The Voice of the Devil'

The devil's voice continues Blake's argument, exposing the destructive falsity of the conventional dualistic vision of mankind: the split between body and soul, the physical and the spiritual. Blake presents instead a model of human nature – of creation as a whole, in fact – which recognises the physical as an important if limited part of the whole entity.

The restraint of physical desires, then, far from being a positive virtue and evidence of a strong moral character, is seen as an indication of the weakness of the desires in question. As Blake fully realised, this position was deliberately provocative to conventional wisdom.

- Is this 'Voice' Blake's own? Are there any other possibilities?

'A Memorable Fancy'

The phrase itself is a deliberate distortion of the 'Memorable Relations' presented by Swedenborg in his *Treatise Concerning Heaven and Hell*, and presents vividly the implications of Blake's views: what **he** sees as genius, the angels of respectable opinion see as 'torment and insanity'. It is perhaps small wonder that many in Blake's time felt the poet to be on the verge of insanity.

- What do you make of the final lines? Aim to represent this idea in pictorial terms.

The Voice of the Devil

All Bibles or sacred codes have been the causes of the following errors:

1. That man has two real existing principles, viz: a body and a soul.
2. That energy, called evil, is alone from the body;   5 and that reason, called good, is alone from the soul.
3. That God will torment man in eternity for following his energies.

But the following contraries to these are true:

1. Man has no body distinct from his soul; for that   10
called body is a portion of soul discerned by the five
senses, the chief inlets of soul in this age.

2. Energy is the only life, and is from the body; and
reason is the bound or outward circumference of
energy.   15

3. Energy is eternal delight.

Those who restrain desire, do so because theirs is weak
enough to be restrained; and the restrainer or reason
usurps its place and governs the unwilling.

And being restrained, it by degrees becomes passive,   20
till it is only the shadow of desire.

A Memorable Fancy

As I was walking among the fires of Hell, delighted
with the enjoyments of genius, which to angels look
like torment and insanity, I collected some of their
proverbs; thinking that as the sayings used in a nation
mark its character, so the Proverbs of Hell show the   5
nature of infernal wisdom better than any description
of buildings or garments.

When I came home: on the abyss of the five senses,
where a flat-sided steep frowns over the present world,
I saw a mighty devil folded in black clouds, hovering   10
on the sides of the rock: with corroding fires he wrote
the following sentence now perceived by the minds of
men, and read by them on earth:

How do you know but ev'ry bird that cuts the airy
way, Is an immense world of delight, clos'd by your   15
senses five?

'Proverbs of Hell'

As promised in the 'Memorable Fancy', Blake now presents the 'Proverbs of Hell', many of which are deliberately provocative.

◆ *Activities and approaches*

1 Choose several of these proverbs and use them as morals to your own fables, which you could write or dramatise.

2 See if you can attach a selection of the proverbs to various of the *Songs of Innocence and of Experience*, explaining how they are appropriate and how they might amplify the meaning of the poems themselves.

3 Some of the proverbs certainly set out to shock. Take, for example, 'Sooner murder an infant in its cradle than nurse unacted desires'. How might the proverb be read? Try to focus on the meaning and associations of the word 'nurse' in deciding this question.

4 Select an appropriate proverb and use it as the motion for a debate on its rightness or otherwise.

5 Choose five proverbs with which you agree, and five with which you disagree. Are they evenly balanced? How sympathetic do you find yourself to any of Blake's views as presented here?

Proverbs of Hell

In seed time learn, in harvest teach, in winter enjoy.
Drive your cart and your plough over the bones of the
dead.
The road of excess leads to the palace of wisdom.
Prudence is a rich, ugly old maid courted by
incapacity.
He who desires but acts not, breeds pestilence. 5
The cut worm forgives the plough.
Dip him in the river who loves water.
A fool sees not the same tree that a wise man sees.
He whose face gives no light, shall never become a star.
Eternity is in love with the productions of time. 10
The busy bee has no time for sorrow.
The hours of folly are measured by the clock; but of
wisdom, no clock can measure.
All wholesome food is caught without a net or a trap.
Bring out number, weight and measure in a year of
dearth.
No bird soars too high, if he soars with his own wings. 15
A dead body revenges not injuries.
The most sublime act is to set another before you.
If the fool would persist in his folly he would become
wise.
Folly is the cloak of knavery.
Shame is pride's cloak. 20
Prisons are built with stones of law, brothels with
bricks of religion.
The pride of the peacock is the glory of God.
The lust of the goat is the bounty of God.
The wrath of the lion is the wisdom of God.
The nakedness of woman is the work of God. 25
Excess of sorrow laughs. Excess of joy weeps.
The roaring of lions, the howling of wolves, the raging
of the stormy sea, and the destructive sword, are
portions of eternity, too great for the eye of man.

The fox condemns the trap, not himself.
Joys impregnate. Sorrows bring forth.
Let man wear the fell of the lion, woman the fleece of   30
the sheep.
The bird a nest, the spider a web, man friendship.
The selfish, smiling fool, and the sullen, frowning fool
shall be both thought wise, that they may be a rod.
What is now proved was once only imagined.
The rat, the mouse, the fox, the rabbit watch the roots;
the lion, the tyger, the horse, the elephant watch the
fruits.
The cistern contains: the fountain overflows.   35
One thought fills immensity.
Always be ready to speak your mind, and a base man
will avoid you.
Everything possible to be believed is an image of truth.
The eagle never lost so much time as when he sub-
mitted to learn of the crow.
The fox provides for himself but God provides for the   40
lion.
Think in the morning. Act in the noon. Eat in the
evening. Sleep in the night.
He who has suffered you to impose on him, knows
you.
As the plough follows words, so God rewards prayers.
The tygers of wrath are wiser than the horses of
instruction.
Expect poison from the standing water.   45
You never know what is enough unless you know
what is more than enough.
Listen to the fool's reproach! It is a kingly title!
The eyes of fire, the nostrils of air, the mouth of water,
the beard of earth.
The weak in courage is strong in cunning.
The apple tree never asks the beech how he shall grow;   50
nor the lion, the horse, how he shall take his prey.
The thankful receiver bears a plentiful harvest.
If others had not been foolish, we should be so.

The soul of sweet delight can never be defiled.
When thou seest an eagle, thou seest a portion of
genius; lift up thy head!
As the caterpillar chooses the fairest leaves to lay her   55
eggs on, so the priest lays his curse on the fairest joys.
To create a little flower is the labour of ages.
Damn braces: Bless relaxes.
The best wine is the oldest, the best water the newest.
Prayers plough not! Praises reap not!
Joys laugh not! Sorrows weep not!   60
The head sublime, the heart pathos, the genitals
beauty, the hands and feet proportion.
As the air to a bird or the sea to a fish, so is contempt
to the contemptible.
The crow wished everything was black, the owl that
everything was white.
Exuberance is beauty.
If the lion was advised by the fox, he would be   65
cunning.
Improvement makes straight roads; but the crooked
roads without improvement are roads of genius.
Sooner murder an infant in its cradle than nurse
unacted desires.
Where man is not, nature is barren.
Truth can never be told so as to be understood, and
not be believed.
Enough! or too much.   70

The Marriage of Heaven and Hell continues with other 'Memorable Fancies', culminating in this statement of belief. The following activities and approaches refer to all of the extracts printed here from *The Marriage of Heaven and Hell*.

✦ *Activities and approaches*

1 Explain in your words how 'the whole creation will ... appear infinite and holy, whereas it now appears finite and corrupt'. Focus on how 'sensual enjoyment' may fit into this process. Are you reminded of any of the *Songs of Innocence and of Experience*?

2 Why do you think that Aldous Huxley, writing in the 1930s about his experiences with the hallucinogenic drug mescalin, entitled his books after Blake: *The Doors of Perception* and *Heaven and Hell*? Similarly, why did Jim Morrison call his 1960s rock band 'The Doors'?

3 The image of the cavern, in which man has imprisoned himself, is an ancient one, stemming at least from Plato, an influential philosopher of Ancient Greece. What might the 'narrow chinks' signify? Do you find this a powerful image?

4 'Opposition is true friendship'. Discuss whether this makes any sense, and if it relates to any of Blake's poems.

5 What do you make of 'One Law for the Lion and Ox is Oppression'? Is it an argument for unequal treatment, or a plea to respect differences between individuals? Present a short mime to elucidate either or both interpretations.

6 'For every thing that lives is holy'. Discuss whether this is a sound guide to live by, and if it is a fitting end to *The Marriage of Heaven and Hell*.

Memorable Fancies

The ancient tradition that the world will be consumed in fire at the end of six thousand years is true, as I have heard from Hell.

For the cherub with his flaming sword is hereby commanded to leave his guard at the tree of life; and when he does, the whole creation will be consumed and appear infinite and holy, whereas it now appears finite and corrupt. 5

This will come to pass by an improvement of sensual enjoyment. 10

But first the notion that man has a body distinct from his soul is to be expunged; this I shall do by printing in the infernal method, by corrosives, which in Hell are salutary and medicinal, melting apparent surfaces away, and displaying the infinite which was hid. 15

If the doors of perception were cleansed everything would appear to man as it is, infinite.

For man has closed himself up, till he sees all things through narrow chinks of his cavern.

Opposition is true friendship. 20

One Law for the Lion and Ox is Oppression.

For everything that lives is holy.

'Motto to The Songs of Innocence and of Experience'

This poem was never included in *Songs of Innocence and of Experience*, but was written at around the same time, before the addition of 'Experience' to 'Innocence'.

- What does the poem tell us about Blake's views on innocence and experience?
- Why was it not included in the 'Songs' themselves?

◆ *Activity*

Create a cluster diagram with this 'Motto' in the centre and lines reaching out to specific quotations from *Songs of Innocence and of Experience*.

'The Smile'

Similarly, this poem relates directly to some of the 'Songs', and perhaps to *The Marriage of Heaven and Hell*.

- What are Blake's feelings on the various facial expressions mentioned? What sort of smiles and frowns are these?

◆ *Activity*

Arrange a collage of pictures of facial expressions with the poem as centrepiece. Can you find any pictorial representations of the final smile with its powerfully healing qualities?

Motto to the Songs of Innocence and of Experience

The good are attracted by men's perceptions,
And think not for themselves –
Till experience teaches them to catch
And to cage the fairies and elves.

And then the knave begins to snarl,   5
And the hypocrite to howl –
And all his good friends show their private ends,
And the eagle is known from the owl.

The Smile

There is a smile of love,
And there is a smile of deceit;
And there is a smile of smiles
In which these two smiles meet.

And there is a frown of hate,   5
And there is a frown of disdain;
And there is a frown of frowns
Which you strive to forget in vain,

For it sticks in the heart's deep core,
And it sticks in the deep backbone;   10
And no smile that ever was smiled,
But only one smile alone

That betwixt the cradle and grave
It only once smiled can be;
But when it once is smiled   15
There's an end to all misery.

Extract from a letter to Rev. Dr. Trusler, 1799

The Reverend John Trusler was an occasional customer for Blake's art, and a conventional Christian educated at Westminster School and Cambridge University. A prolific writer and energetic patron of the arts, he was also a wealthy and influential figure unused to artists in his employ having and sticking to their own ideas. Having commissioned Blake to paint depictions of 'Malevolence' and 'Benevolence' with very clear and explicit instructions, Trusler was in no mood to comply with Blake's own very individual ideas on the project, writing, somewhat tersely, to Blake: 'Your Fancy ... seems to be in the other world or the World of Spirits, which accords not with my intentions, which, whilst living in This World, Wish to follow the Nature of it'. The extract printed here is Blake's reply to Trusler's comments, and it seems to encapsulate Blake's most profound beliefs.

- What point is Blake making about 'Visions of Eternity'?
- What are Blake's views on the nature of 'This World'?
- How are 'Nature' and 'Imagination' related here?
- 'As a man is, so he sees'. What do you make of this formulation? Is it true, in your own experience?
- Relate any of the points made to characters from 'Songs of Innocence'. Is there any kinship?

✦ *Activity*

Write a further reply from Rev. Trusler to Blake, taking issue in detail with the various points Blake makes, and remembering it is you who is employing the impoverished engraver, not the other way round.

Extract from a letter to Rev. Trusler, 1799

Fun I love but too much Fun is of all things the most loath-
som. Mirth is better than Fun, & Happiness is better than
Mirth. I feel that a Man may be happy in This World. And I
know that This World Is a World of Imagination & Vision.
I see Every thing I paint In This World, but Every body does   5
not see alike. To the Eyes of a Miser a Guinea is far more
beautiful than the Sun, & a bag worn with the use of Money
has more beautiful proportions than a Vine filled with
Grapes. The tree which moves some to tears of joy is in the   10
Eyes of others only a Green thing which stands in the way.
Some see Nature all Ridicule & Deformity, & by these I
shall not regulate my proportions; & some scarce see Nature
at all. But to the Eyes of the Man of Imagination, Nature is
Imagination itself. As a man is, so he sees. As the Eye is   15
formed, such are its Powers. You certainly Mistake, when
you say that the Visions of Fancy are not to be found in This
World. To Me This World is all One continued Vision of
Fancy or Imagination, & I feel Flatter'd when I am told so.
What is it sets Homer, Virgil & Milton in so high a rank of   20
Art? Why is the Bible more Entertaining & Instructive than
any other book? Is it not because they are addressed to the
Imagination, which is Spiritual Sensation, & but mediately
to the Understanding or Reason? Such is True Painting, and
such was alone valued by the Greeks & the best modern   25
Artists. Consider what Lord Bacon says: 'Sense sends over to
Imagination before Reason have judged, & Reason sends
over to Imagination before the Decree can be acted.' See
Advancement of Learning, Part 2 P. 47 of first Edition.

But I am happy to find a Great Majority of Fellow   30
Mortals who can Elucidate My Visions, & Particularly
they have been Elucidated by Children, who have taken a
greater delight in contemplating my Pictures than I even
hoped. Neither Youth nor Childhood is Folly or
Incapacity. Some Children are Fools & so are some Old   35
Men. But There is a vast Majority on the side of
Imagination or Spiritual Sensation.

'The Mental Traveller'

This long, complex poem was written rather later than the *Songs of Innocence and of Experience* or *The Marriage of Heaven and Hell*, dating approximately from 1804. It is possible and perhaps helpful to relate the ideas and events of the poem to the earlier books, not least in order to make them more accessible.

- Trace carefully the events of the poem. What, in your words, actually happens? Try to gain an impression rather than a close understanding of every detail, at least to start with.

- What elements of innocence and experience are there in the poem? Show how the two qualities interact throughout the poem.

- Look at the imagery here. Are there any echoes of earlier poems? Are there new elements? What might they signify?

- Sex is often made explicit in this poem. Why do you think this is? Are sexual issues crucial to your understanding of the poem as a whole?

✦ *Activities and approaches*

1 The structure of the poem and its narrative sequence are circular, that is, the ending echoes the beginning. Discuss whether this makes for optimism or pessimism.

2 The subject matter is suitable for a surrealist film. Imagine you are directing, and construct a series of 'storyboard' sketches to present the poem imaginatively.

3 Re-write the story from the Babe's viewpoint, looking back on the events from adulthood.

The Mental Traveller

I travelled through a land of men,
A land of men and women too,
And heard and saw such dreadful things
As cold earth wanderers never knew.

For there the babe is born in joy   5
That was begotten in dire woe,
Just as we reap in joy the fruit
Which we in bitter tears did sow;

And if the babe is born a boy
He's given to a woman old,   10
Who nails him down upon a rock,
Catches his shrieks in cups of gold.

She binds iron thorns around his head,
She pierces both his hands and feet,
She cuts his heart out at his side   15
To make it feel both cold & heat.

Her fingers number every nerve
Just as a miser counts his gold;
She lives upon his shrieks and cries –
And she grows young as he grows old,   20

Till he becomes a bleeding youth
And she becomes a virgin bright;
Then he rends up his manacles
And binds her down for his delight.

He plants himself in all her nerves   25
Just as a husbandman his mould,
And she becomes his dwelling-place
And garden, fruitful seventyfold.

An aged shadow soon he fades,
Wandering round an earthly cot,   30
Full filled all with gems and gold
Which he by industry had got.

And these are the gems of the human soul:
The rubies and pearls of a lovesick eye,
The countless gold of the aching heart,   35
The martyr's groan, and the lover's sigh.

They are his meat, they are his drink:
He feeds the beggar and the poor
And the wayfaring traveller;
For ever open is his door.   40

His grief is their eternal joy,
They make the roofs and walls to ring –
Till from the fire on the hearth
A little female babe does spring!

And she is all of solid fire   45
And gems and gold, that none his hand
Dares stretch to touch her baby form,
Or wrap her in his swaddling-band.

But she comes to the man she loves,
If young or old, or rich or poor;   50
They soon drive out the aged host,
A beggar at another's door.

He wanders weeping far away
Until some other take him in;
Oft blind and age-bent, sore distressed,   55
Until he can a maiden win.

And to allay his freezing age
The poor man takes her in his arms:
The cottage fades before his sight,
The garden and its lovely charms;   60

The guests are scattered through the land
(For the eye altering, alters all);
The senses roll themselves in fear,
And the flat earth becomes a ball,

The stars, sun, moon, all shrink away –   65
   A desert vast without a bound,
   And nothing left to eat or drink
   And a dark desert all around.

   The honey of her infant lips,
The bread and wine of her sweet smile,   70
   The wild game of her roving eye
   Does him to infancy beguile.

For as he eats and drinks he grows
   Younger and younger every day;
   And on the desert wild they both   75
   Wander in terror and dismay.

Like the wild stag she flees away;
Her fear plants many a thicket wild,
While he pursues her night & day,
   By various arts of love beguiled,   80

   By various arts of love and hate,
   Till the wide desert planted o'er
   With labyrinths of wayward love,
Where roams the lion, wolf and boar,

Till he becomes a wayward babe   85
   And she a weeping woman old.
   Then many a lover wanders here,
The sun and stars are nearer rolled,

The trees bring forth sweet ecstasy
   To all who in the desert roam,   90
   Till many a city there is built,
And many a pleasant shepherd's home.

But when they find the frowning babe
Terror strikes through the region wide;
They cry, 'The Babe! the Babe is born!'   95
   And flee away on every side.

For who dare touch the frowning form
His arm is withered to its root,
Lions, boars, wolves, all howling flee
And every tree does shed its fruit;   100

And none can touch that frowning form,
Except it be a woman old;
She nails him down upon the rock,
And all is done as I have told.

'Auguries of Innocence'

Like 'The Mental Traveller', this poem dates from the early nineteenth century. Again, there is much that is relevant to the *Songs of Innocence and of Experience*. The opening quatrain is one of Blake's most famous expressions of his profound belief in the liberating power of vision and imagination, and seems in itself to encapsulate the quality of innocence.

✦ *Activities and approaches*

1 Discuss whether it is possible to match images from the poem to any of those in *Songs of Innocence and of Experience*.

2 Use quotations from the poem for a dramatic or visual presentation on cruelty to animals, emphasising the effect not only on animals but also on the people responsible.

3 Represent in picture form the opening quatrain, or a part of it, to stress the power of the imagination.

4 Use lines 55–62 as a subtitle for writing a children's story illustrating the idea expressed. Consider whether this sounds like the sort of advice a kindly adult from 'Innocence' might give.

5 Examine lines 85–90. Discuss the positive and negative aspects of encouraging children to doubt. Then, present a reasoned dialogue between Blake and a schoolteacher who disagrees with him and encourages doubt as a step towards knowledge.

6 Present a chanted or rhythmically musical performance of any section of the 'Auguries'.

7 Dramatise lines 111–12 to stress either the positive or the negative aspects of being 'in a passion' as opposed to controlling the passion 'in you'.

8 Consider how one sees 'Through the eye' (l. 126) and how this idea is central to Blake's philosophy.

9 Interpret the last four lines as a dream sequence using mime and music to contrast night and day, darkness and light.

Auguries of Innocence

To see a world in a grain of sand
And a heaven in a wild flower,
Hold infinity in the palm of your hand
And eternity in an hour.
A robin redbreast in a cage   5
Puts all Heaven in a rage,
A dove-house filled with doves and pigeons
Shudders Hell through all its regions.
A dog starved at his master's gate
Predicts the ruin of the state.   10
A horse misused upon the road
Calls to Heaven for human blood.
Each outcry of the hunted hare
A fibre from the brain does tear.
A skylark wounded in the wing,   15
A cherubim does cease to sing.
The gamecock° clipped and armed for fight
Does the rising sun affright.
Every wolf's and lion's howl
Raises from Hell a human soul.   20
The wild deer wandering here and there
Keeps the human soul from care.
The lamb misused breeds public strife,
And yet forgives the butcher's knife.
The bat that flits at close of eve   25
Has left the brain that won't believe.
The owl that calls upon the night
Speaks the unbeliever's fright.
He who shall hurt the little wren
Shall never be beloved by men.   30
He who the ox to wrath has moved
Shall never be by woman loved.
The wanton boy that kills the fly
Shall feel the spider's enmity.
He who torments the chafer's° sprite   35
Weaves a bower in endless night.

The caterpillar on the leaf
Repeats to thee thy mother's grief.
Kill not the moth nor butterfly,
For the Last Judgement draweth nigh.   40
He who shall train the horse to war
  Shall never pass the polar bar.°
The beggar's dog and widow's cat –
Feed them and thou wilt grow fat.
The gnat that sings his summer's song   45
Poison gets from slander's tongue.
The poison of the snake and newt
  Is the sweat of envy's foot;
  The poison of the honey bee
  Is the artist's jealousy.   50
The prince's robes and beggar's rags
Are toadstools on the miser's bags.
A truth that's told with bad intent
Beats all the lies you can invent.
  It is right it should be so;   55
Man was made for joy and woe,
And when this we rightly know
Through the world we safely go.
  Joy and woe are woven fine,
  A clothing for the soul divine.   60
  Under every grief and pine
  Runs a joy with silken twine.
The babe is more than swaddling bands:
Throughout all these human lands
Tools were made and born were hands –   65
  Every farmer understands.
  Every tear from every eye
  Becomes a babe in eternity;
  This is caught by females bright
  And returned to its own delight.   70
The bleat, the bark, bellow and roar
Are waves that beat on heaven's shore.
The babe that weeps the rod beneath
Writes *Revenge!* in realms of death.

The beggar's rags fluttering in air   75
    Does to rags the heavens tear.
The soldier armed with sword and gun
    Palsied strikes the summer's sun.
The poor man's farthing is worth more
    Than all the gold on Afric's shore.   80
One mite° wrung from the labourer's hands
    Shall buy and sell the miser's lands;
    Or if protected from on high
Does that whole nation sell and buy.
    He who mocks the infant's faith   85
    Shall be mocked in age and death.
He who shall teach the child to doubt
    The rotting grave shall ne'er get out.
    He who respects the infant's faith
    Triumphs over hell and death.   90
The child's toys and the old man's reasons
    Are the fruits of the two seasons.
    The questioner who sits so sly
    Shall never know how to reply.
    He who replies to words of doubt   95
Doth put the light of knowledge out.
    The strongest poison ever known
    Came from Caesar's laurel crown.
    Nought can deform the human race
    Like to the armour's iron brace.   100
When gold and gems adorn the plough
    To peaceful arts shall envy bow.
    A riddle, or the cricket's cry,
    Is to doubt a fit reply.
The emmet's° inch and eagle's mile   105
    Make lame philosophy to smile.
He who doubts from what he sees
Will ne'er believe, do what you please.
If the sun and moon should doubt
    They'd immediately go out.   110
To be in a passion you good may do,
    But no good if a passion is in you.

The whore and gambler by the state
Licenced build that nation's fate.
The harlot's cry from street to street   115
Shall weave old England's winding sheet;
The winner's shout, the loser's curse
Dance before dead England's hearse.
Every night and every morn
Some to misery are born;   120
Every morn and every night
Some are born to sweet delight.
Some are born to sweet delight,
Some are born to endless night.
We are led to believe a lie   125
When we see not through the eye,
Which was born in a night to perish in a night,
When the soul slept in beams of light.
God appears and God is light
To those poor souls who dwell in night,   130
But does a human form display
To those who dwell in realms of day.

17 'The gamecock' refers to the barbaric 'sport' of cock fighting.
35 'chafer' is a beetle.
42 'the polar bar' implies the passage to another, better world.
81 'mite' refers to an almost valueless coin.
105 'emmet' is an ant.

GENERAL APPROACHES AND ACTIVITIES

This section looks at more general 'ways in' to Blake's writing, using, as often as possible, his own words as guidance. There are five major areas of concern and study in the appreciation of Blake's work, which have been implicit throughout the activities and approaches relating to each of the poems studied. In this section, they are more directly relevant, and you should try to use them as further guides in the rewarding process of understanding Blake, his age and his work.

◆

Who was Blake and why did he write these poems?

Blake's life

Not a great deal is known about Blake's life; perhaps little needs to be. Born in 1757 into a Christian but Non-Conformist London family dominated by his hosier father, Blake was to live all but two of his seventy years in London. Apparently he displayed early in life a vivid and robust imagination, and a remarkable artistic talent: the former was met by incomprehension, but the latter must have attracted some family sympathy for he attended a Strand drawing school from the age of ten. In 1772, he became an apprentice engraver, his subsequent means of livelihood, and ten years later he married Catherine, or Kate, Boucher. Early promise – he set up a print shop with his beloved younger brother Robert – was swiftly shattered by business failure and Robert's death in 1787, and for the rest of his life Blake relied on various patrons to make a living.

He was deeply involved in radical politics and religion, at least until his apparent disillusionment with political revolution and with the Swedenborgian New Church. This led him increasingly towards a highly personal stance ill-suited to any sort of organised movement. Blake never knew commercial success or wide recognition, and his attempt to put down roots in the Sussex seaside village of Felpham between 1800 and 1802 ended in failure. His creations became ever more complex – some would say obscure – and he frequently quarrelled with his few friends, although during his last years he was intensely admired as 'The Interpreter' by a group of young mystical painters including Samuel Palmer. The bare facts of an outwardly rather unsuccessful life belie the true nature of Blake's accomplishment; but here, you must make up your own mind, after studying his work and reading this time chart:

1757	Born 28 November, Broad Street, London.
1767	Robert, William's favourite brother, born. Attends William Parr's drawing school, London.
1772	Apprenticed to James Basire, engraver.
1776	American Declaration of Independence.
1779	Apprenticeship completed. Student at the Royal Academy.
1780	Gordon Riots; witnesses burning of Newgate Prison.
1782	Marries Catherine (Kate) Boucher.
1783	*Poetical Sketches* printed privately.
1784	Sets up print shop. Exhibits at the Royal Academy. *An Island in the Moon* written, including some poems later to appear in *Songs of Innocence*. Death of Blake's father James.
1785	End of print shop partnership.
1787	Death of brother Robert, from consumption.
1788–89	Involved in the Swedenborgian New Church.
1789	French Revolution. *Songs of Innocence* engraved.
1791–92	Thomas Paine's *Rights of Man* published.
1792	Death of Blake's mother, Catherine.

1792	Completion of *The Marriage of Heaven and Hell*. Mary Wollstonecraft's *Vindication of the Rights of Women* published.
1793	Execution of Louis XVI; war with France. Godwin's *Enquiry Concerning Political Justice* published.
1794	*Songs of Innocence and of Experience* published.
1798	Wordsworth and Coleridge publish *Lyrical Ballads*.
1799	Combination Acts prohibit trades unions.
1800–1803	Lives in Felpham, employed by Hayley.
1803	Returns to London. Acquittal in court on charge of assault and sedition.
1804	Napoleon crowns himself Emperor.
1809	Exhibition of paintings; attacked in *The Examiner* as 'the wild effusions' of 'an unfortunate lunatic'.
1810	Abolition of British slave trade: limited effect.
1811	Outbreak of Luddite rebellions.
1809–12	Work on prophetic books *Milton*, *Vala* and *Jerusalem*.
1815	End of Napoleonic Wars. Economic depression.
1815–17	Designs for Wedgwood china; poverty.
1819	Peterloo massacre: peak of political reaction.
1824	Meets Samuel Palmer: start of a fruitful relationship with a group of artists known as the 'Shoreham Ancients'.
1827	12 August 6:00 pm: Blake dies.
1831	Death of Blake's wife, Catherine.

Blake and politics

Inescapable here is the political turmoil of Blake's age, and its impact on Blake's work. Blake himself was drawn towards radicalism in politics – a belief in freedom of the individual within a democratic social structure – born of an incisive, deeply-felt critique of the unchristian, repressive nature of the society he lived in. 'To defend the Bible in this year 1798 would cost a man his life. The Beast and the Whore rule without control', he wrote privately, and as an artist he held that 'a warlike state never can produce art. It will rob and plunder and accumulate in one place and translate and copy and buy and sell and criticise, but not make.' Blake's radicalism attracted the authorities' attention, not least because he associated with such figures as the anarchist thinker William Godwin, Mary Wollstonecraft – an important early feminist who married Godwin – and Thomas Paine, whose *Rights of Man* became a significant influence on revolutionary thought.

Blake was not a supporter of establishment politics. In his *Public Address* of about 1810, Blake wrote:

> I am really sorry to see my countrymen trouble themselves about politics. If men were wise, the most arbitrary Princes could not hurt them. If they are not wise, the freest government is compelled to be a tyranny. Princes appear to me to be fools. Houses of Commons and Houses of Lords appear to me to be fools; they seem to me to be something else besides human life.

This passage suggests Blake was abandoning politics, at least in terms of its power to reform political institutions, and to provide the solution to political ills. This was not surprising, given the transformation of revolutionary France into Napoleon's war-like empire. In a sense, though, his radicalism is still there, only deeper: concerned with a total revolution of human nature.

In Blake's time, politics was inextricably mixed with religious belief, in a way that is difficult for us, living in a more agnostic culture and age, to appreciate. For Blake, the link was especially potent: both are vital if this total revolution is to occur, and to understand the man and his work – who exactly was he and why did he write? – you must come to terms with both.

Blake and religion

Blake considered himself on intimate terms with Heaven and Hell, yet his most forceful criticism is often reserved for the Church. His Christianity is founded on an image of Christ as energetically rebellious, as opposed to the more usual and conservative worship of a far-off, idealised divinity. As he wrote, addressing conventional Christians in 'The Everlasting Gospel' of 1818:

> The vision of Christ that thou dost see
> Is my vision's greatest enemy.

Blake sometimes describes this rebellious spirit of Christ with an almost colloquial tone, suggesting personal intimacy: 'First God Almighty comes with a thump on the head. Then Jesus Christ comes with a balm to heal it.' Blake held that 'Man must and will have some religion: if he has not the religion of Jesus, he will have the religion of Satan', but for him the religion of Jesus was radical and personally experienced through the imagination. For him, this continued the tradition whereby 'The Hebrew Bible and the Gospel of Jesus are ... eternal vision or imagination of all that exists.'

✦ Activities

1 Choose a volunteer to role-play Blake himself, placing him in the hot-seat. What questions would you ask him? You could extend this exercise to include others who knew him – provided you research thoroughly. His wife Kate, younger brother Robert, parents, patrons George Cumberland, William Hayley and Thomas Butts, fellow artists Henry Fuseli and John Flaxman, and disciples John Linnell and Samuel Palmer, could all be involved.

2 Examine the time chart of Blake's life and times on pages 127–8 for what it tells you about the nature of the age he lived in, and for what impressions you receive of the man himself. Carefully research those areas mentioned which may be only vaguely familiar to you in order to broaden your knowledge of William Blake and his background – biographical, political, artistic, literary and religious – and compile a short guide for future students of Blake using this information.

3 Consider and debate the conflict between Blake's beliefs and those of the official Church, and the relevance of his characters and symbols in the poems to this conflict.

◆

What type of texts are these poems and engravings?

To pose this question is to address the very Blakean concern about the whole nature of human creativity, and it can be argued that whatever else Blake might be writing about, he is always grappling with this facet of the human character.

The poetic form

It is significant that Blake chose poetry and visual art as his twin media: both appeal directly to the visual imagination. The language of poetry is condensed, powerful and evocative: language working hard. In Blake's poetry there is a forceful directness of approach, and his chosen style of formal simplicity, usually based on the four-line stanza (the quatrain), is well suited to this directness. The 'Songs of Experience', especially, often sound like traditional English folk songs in the powerful simplicity of the rhythmic and rhyme structure. But this is only part of the story, for there is profound complexity also in Blake's vision: ideas often at odds with everyday, conventional modes of thought. Blake insisted on firmness of outline, both in his poetry and his art, precisely because formal structure would best allow unfamiliar thoughts and feelings to affect his readers, whereas a more experimental form may well have served only to cloud the issues. Blake's creativity is always concerned with clarity, not mystery – which he hated.

Throughout Blake's work, creativity is valued and defended intensely, as his own creation, the character Los, proclaims in *Jerusalem*:

> I must create a system or be enslaved by another man's.
> I will not reason or compare: my business is to create.

Romanticism

Blake was not alone in addressing the problems and opportunities of creativity – they were, in fact, central concerns of what became known as Romanticism. Blake is often regarded as a key figure in the first wave of English Romanticism, in terms of both his pictorial art and his poetry. Romanticism, however, was never a clearly-defined movement, and most of the Romantics were not aware of the term at all, and would have probably objected to being grouped with other 'exponents'. Romanticism, then, is largely a label used with the benefit of hindsight; nevertheless it does seem to be helpful in denoting a certain movement in human consciousness which gathered momentum towards the end of the eighteenth century, and which has never left us since. As such, it is useful briefly to explore Romanticism, and Blake's relationship to its main characteristics.

In certain crucial ways, Blake's ideas and artistic practice may be seen as distinctly Romantic: political radicalism; emphasis on the individual imagination; the placing of feeling above reason; a love of 'Gothic' as distinct from 'Classical' form; the elevation of art into a liberating force; and the refusal to compromise individual ideals. Many other Romantic figures, however, professed an almost pantheistic love of nature; here, Wordsworth is perhaps the best-known example amongst English Romantic poets, and, interestingly, some of Blake's marginal notes on Wordsworth's poetry have survived. The following quotations are taken from them, written in 1826. Wordsworth wrote:

> And I could wish my days to be
> Bound each to each by natural piety.

Upon which Blake commented: 'There is no such thing as natural piety because the natural man is at enmity with God.' Some pages further on, Wordsworth's lines:

> Influence of natural objects
> In calling forth and strengthening the imagination
> In boyhood and early youth

attracted Blake's indignation: 'Natural objects always did and now do weaken, deaden and obliterate imagination in me. Wordsworth must know that what he writes valuable is not to be found in nature.' There is a fundamental distinction between the two attitudes here. Blake uses natural imagery throughout his work, but always as symbolic of human concerns and rarely for its own sake as purely descriptive.

✦ Activities

1 Look again at the illustrations of Blake's poems, and research his other paintings and engravings. Consider the relationship between his poetry and his pictorial art, discussing whether the one complements the other, or whether they are better experienced separately.

2 Reconsider the forms of Blake's poetry, particularly the rhythm and rhyme schemes, and discuss whether the meaning is enhanced by the poetic form chosen. When examining these aspects of the work, it is as well to remember that the poems often come to life best when read aloud as a performance, individually or chorally. Choose contrasting examples, such as 'The Echoing Green' (p. 13), 'The Little Black Boy' (p. 21), 'A Little Girl Lost' (pp. 53–4), 'The Sick Rose' (p. 63) and 'The Voice of the Ancient Bard' (p. 84).

◆

How were the poems produced?

The production process

For Blake the craftsman engraver, concerned with earning an often precarious living in a shrinking market, creativity was no abstract, idealised matter. Having served his long apprenticeship under James Basire, Blake worked as an independent engraver throughout his life, developing skills appropriate to his craft. The process of engraving poetry and illustration together was apparently suggested by the spirit of his beloved and deeply-mourned brother Robert, who, according to a contemporary account by one J. T. Smith, came to Blake's aid, when Blake

> had deeply perplexed himself as to the mode of accomplishing the publication of his illustrated songs, without their being subject to the expense of letter-press, his brother Robert stood before him in one of his visionary imaginations, and so decidedly directed him in the way in which he ought to proceed, that he immediately followed his advice, by writing his poetry, and drawing his marginal subjects of imbellishments in outline upon the copper-plate with an impervious liquid, and then eating the plain parts or lights away with aqua fortis considerably below them, so that the outlines were left as a stereotype.

Visionary assistance and practical concerns for saving money happily coincided here, although the process never led to the prosperity Blake hoped for. Particularly significant is the integration of design and words, with the hand colouring, often by his wife Kate, lending individuality to each product.

Blake's views on the production process, and on art generally, reflect his entire philosophy; thus:

> The great and golden rule of art, as well as of life, is this: that the more distinct, sharp and wiry the bounding line, the more perfect the work of art, and the less keen and sharp, the greater is the evidence of weak imitation, plagiarism and bungling.

Imitation he held in contempt: 'He who copies does not execute.' The idea of distinctive individuality is central to Blake's art, and derives directly from his practical experience as a craftsman engraver. The 'how?' is for Blake no mere means to an end, but an integral part of the end itself, and thus deserving celebration and care: 'Passion and expression are beauty itself', he maintained.

Role of the imagination
Imagination is for Blake the key to creativity, and the essence of what constitutes humanity: 'The true vine of eternity, the human imagination.' The images and symbols are provided by nature, but are transformed by the imagination. Blake acknowledges that 'It is impossible to think without images of somewhat on earth', but these images become powerfully and meaningfully human only when they enter consciousness. As Blake wrote to his rather more prosaic patron Thomas Butts:

> Each grain of sand,
> Every stone on the land,
> Each rock and each hill,
> Each fountain and rill,
> Each herb and each tree,

Mountain, hill, earth and sea,
Cloud, meteor and star,
Are men seen afar.

It is through a deliberate and conscious act of mind that the
power of the imagination, which children take for granted in
the state of innocence, may be recovered in adulthood:

> The nature of visionary fancy, or imagination, is very little
> known, and the eternal nature and permanence of its ever exist-
> ant images is considered as less permanent than the things of
> vegetative and generative nature; yet the oak dies as well as the
> lettuce, but its eternal image and individuality never dies, but
> renews by its seed; just so the imaginative image returns by the
> seed of contemplative thought.

✦ *Activities*

1 Look again at the various drafts of poems included in this
book. Look for any pattern emerging in the way Blake
actually wrote his poems, and compare Blake's drafting with
that of other writers, including, perhaps, yourself and other
students. Poets whose drafts are relatively easily available
include Wordsworth, Wilfred Owen and T. S. Eliot.

2 Research the history of engraving as a craft and consider
Blake's position in this tradition. Concentrate particularly
on the insistence on a firm boundary outline in all his
illustrations; the individually hand-painted plates with their
subtle differences; and the concern for unity of design and
words in an integrated artistic endeavour.

✦

How does Blake present his various themes?

The central theme examined in this book is that of the relationship between innocence and experience. It is clear that Blake
was concerned with a major re-evaluation of the concept of
innocence, questioning its restricted connotations of sentimen-
tality and nostalgia, and with this, a fresh outlook upon the
meaning of experience. If you consider how Blake presents
innocence and experience in his poetry, you may also discover
the key to his presentation of other subjects and themes, so
fundamental are these areas to Blake's vision. There are various
ways in which Blake uses language to convey his ideas.

Questions and affirmations

Blake himself wrote: 'Unorganised innocence: an impossibility.
Innocence dwells with wisdom, but never with ignorance'
(*Vala* or *The Four Zoas*), suggesting that wisdom lies with
innocence rather than experience. He also implies here that his
presentational method demands skilful organisation precisely
because it is dealing with the elusive subtleties of innocence and
its relationship with experience. From the adult perspective,
people must learn to question the nature of experience and its
lessons of selfishness, before they can recover the use of their
imaginations. So, if you look at the 'Experience' version of
'Holy Thursday' (p. 51), 'The Tiger' (p. 59), 'A Little Boy Lost'
(p. 79), where the questions have an angrily ironic tone, or 'The
Schoolboy' (p. 83), you may see the insistent questions under-
mining the apparent strength of experience. This, in turn,
forces you, the reader, to respond in some way to their lack of
answer. It may be that questions by themselves are not enough,
however, and in poems such as 'London' (p. 73) or 'The
Human Abstract' (p. 75), Blake moves towards affirmations,
intensely critical of the nature of the areas of experience he is
considering. In your own study of Blake's poems, you will need
to evaluate critically the relationship between questions and

affirmations, and there is no better way than by posing your own questions about the material, before providing possible affirmations.

Imagery of the natural world

Consider again the vast range of images of the natural world used by Blake throughout the poems you have studied. These are images apparently derived from Blake's acute observations of nature during his youthful rambles in what is now north London, but was then the rolling countryside of Middlesex. Useful ways of coming to terms with these many images could be to construct a dictionary of symbols and their possible meanings for a newcomer to Blake's poetry, or a diagrammatic and pictorial representation of them. You will need to use examples from the poems themselves, and to consider carefully the appropriateness of each image, asking yourself whether it actually works for your own imagination.

Allusions to Biblical and mythical sources

Blake's innovative and strongly individual reading of the Bible adds a further vital dimension to his work. He wrote in *The Marriage of Heaven and Hell* of converting an angel to his own unconventional reading, adding: 'this angel, who is now become a devil, is my particular friend; we often read the Bible together in its infernal or diabolical sense, which the world shall have if they behave well'. At other times, Blake sought to create his own complex mythology, peopled by creations of his own imagination but sometimes drawing on ancient myths and legends. Look carefully again at some of the Biblical symbols – the lamb, the father, the son, angels and devils, for example – and consider how exactly they are used. In the same way, discuss how mythological themes and characters – the adventures of Lyca, for example, in 'The Little Girl Lost' and 'Found' (pp. 53–6) – are presented by Blake to amplify the meaning of his poetry for you.

Blake's individual voice

Experience, for Blake, all too often means needless suffering. Blake's sympathy for human suffering is one of the most marked features of his writing, whether his reaction is one of quiet comfort or righteous wrath. His presentation of experience is at once compassionate and forceful, for he realised that sympathy is not enough unless it is accompanied by a practical sense of liberation. In this passage, Blake extends compassion to all creation, and the presentation is both direct and subtle:

> It is an easy thing to triumph in the summer's sun
> And in the vintage, and to sing on the wagon loaded with corn.
> It is an easy thing to talk of patience to the afflicted,
> To speak the laws of prudence to the houseless wanderer,
> To listen to the hungry raven's cry in wintry season
> When the red blood is filled with wine and with the marrow
> of lambs.
> It is an easy thing to laugh at the wrathful elements,
> To hear the dog howl at the wintry door, the ox in the
> slaughter house moan;
> To see a god on every wind and a blessing on every blast ...
> It is an easy thing to rejoice in the tents of prosperity:
> Thus could I sing and thus rejoice: but it is not so with me.
>
> (from *Vala* or *The Four Zoas*)

✦ *Activity*

In groups, dramatise several of the poems: they lend themselves impressively to the medium. For example, you might arrange for meetings between characters and symbols. Use drama as the visible outward form of Blake's imagination, including techniques such as mime, dance, tableaux, masks, and hot-seating.

Who reads Blake's work and how is it interpreted?

There are, it sometimes seems, as many interpretations of Blake as there are readers, and the activities and approaches included here are designed to encourage you to make your own responses. Blake is clearly trying to lead his readers somewhere important: not for him the idea of art as a pleasant diversion. He wrote (in *Jerusalem*, his major prophetic book):

> I give you the end of a golden string,
> Only wind it into a ball,
> It will lead you in at Heaven's gate
> Built in Jerusalem's wall.

It is fascinating to consider what his advice might be to us, living two centuries later, for it is possible to interpret the particular nature and meaning of the golden string in different ways – to read the poems differently, in fact – and so arrive at different versions of 'Heaven's gate'. Here is a brief guide to help you consider two opposing perspectives, focusing particularly on the poem 'The Tiger' (p. 59).

The Marxist position

The emphasis here tends to be on Blake as revolutionary socialist, and is presented powerfully by Edward Larrissy, in his *William Blake* (1985). He follows Terry Eagleton's sense of Blake as 'England's greatest revolutionary artist' in his analysis of Blake's critique of the uses and abuses of power:

> Many of Blake's poems are criticisms of oppressive uses of power on many levels, and they imply that there is a link between the use of power when one individual belittles another and the use of power on a large political and economic scale.

Taking this interpretative position with regard to 'The Tiger', it may be that the tiger itself is a symbol of political oppression irreconcilable with the goodness of the lamb. The tiger is apparently all powerful, but in reality – emphasised by the harmless appearance of Blake's illustration – nothing but a paper tiger deserving of a swift overthrow, very much like the ruling class in Blake's Britain.

The mystical position

The mystical interpretation is espoused convincingly in the meticulous research of Kathleen Raine, who has written many books on Blake, and who places Blake firmly in a mystical tradition which transcends time and place:

> Blake has not been my 'subject' but my Master, in the Indian sense of the word … To live by the Imagination is Blake's secret of life … There is nothing outside the Imagination, which is immortal, eternal and boundless.

As far as 'The Tiger' is concerned, the mystical approach may be more likely to highlight the age-old theological question of the nature of evil, symbolised by the tiger, in a universe created by a loving Creator: the maker of the lamb and, by direct connection, the lamb-like spiritual son, Jesus Christ.

Other interpretations of Blake

There are many more possible views of Blake's work. It is possible to read 'The Tiger' for evidence of sexual liberation, and see Blake as a precursor of Sigmund Freud and psychoanalysis in an overriding concern to throw off sexual repression. Or you could read Blake as a liberal humanist, concerned above all with breadth of education in changing the world for the better: this is a stance taken by several critics, for example Stanley Gardner. Northrop Frye takes a structuralist approach, relating Blake to the 'history of his own times' and seeing in the social and economic structure of his age the key to understanding the poet and artist. Another influential critic, E. D. Hirsch, stresses instead Blake's radical Christianity and his formative relationship to Swedenborg (see Further Reading, pages 143–4).

It seems to me in my own reading – but you must decide on yours – that one thing above all is clear: Blake claims the potential for some kind of human liberation through his work:

> If the spectator could enter into these images in his imagination, if he ... could make a friend and companion of one of these images of wonder ... then would he arise from his grave, then would he meet the Lord in the air and then would he be happy. General knowledge is remote knowledge; it is in particulars that wisdom consists and happiness too.
>
> (*Descriptive Catalogue* for 'Vision of the Last Judgement')

The 'images of wonder' are the poems and illustrations, and the underlying purpose of the approaches included in this book is to allow you to enter them into your own imagination.

◆ *Activities*

1 Several, if not all, of Blake's poems are open to conflicting interpretations. Read them aloud, emphasising a particular meaning in your method of reading and intonation to see which 'fits' best.

2 Consider for whom Blake wrote his poems: children; his small circle of friends and patrons; himself; the public at large. Discuss how different people would read Blake's poems in different ways: for example children, his own friends, members of the Church, political opponents, or people from various walks of life in modern times.

3 Apply different interpretive models in close reading of the poems themselves, discussing how different critical viewpoints may lead to different and perhaps opposing readings. You could then go on to role play the various critical positions, focusing on a particular poem, in a 'Critics' Debate' presentation: possible viewpoints could include

those of a political revolutionary, a devout Christian, a liberal humanist, and a clinical psychologist.

4 Think of other people, alive and dead, with similar ideas to Blake, or similar methods of expression. Poets and artists are the most obvious, but think also of singers, songwriters, religious thinkers, psychologists and political writers. Consider especially whether Blake is still relevant today.

◆

FURTHER READING

Facsimiles

Songs of Innocence and of Experience (ed. Keynes, 1967)

The Marriage of Heaven and Hell (ed. Keynes, 1975)

The Notebook of William Blake (ed. Erdman, 1973)

The above editions have scholarly notes and clear introductions. The *Songs* and the *Marriage* particularly show the integrated nature of Blake's art and poetry in accessible form. The originals are to be found in the British Museum.

Complete works

Complete Writings (ed. Keynes, 1966)

The Poetry and Prose (ed. Erdman, 1966)

The two main collections, the latter extensively annotated.

Biographies

M. Wilson, *The Life of William Blake* (Oxford University Press, 1927, revised 1971)

J. King, *William Blake – His Life* (Weidenfeld & Nicolson, 1991: makes use of recent research and is highly accessible)

Criticism

M. Bottrall (ed.), *Songs of Innocence and Experience* (Macmillan Casebook Series, 1970: a very useful collection of material)

J. Bronowski, *William Blake and the Age of Revolution* (Routlege and Kegan Paul, 1972: a useful contextualising study)

M. Ferber, *The Poetry of William Blake* (Penguin Critical Studies Series, 1991: an admirably clear critical introduction, entirely accessible to school students)

S. Gardner, *Blake's 'Innocence and Experience' Retraced* (St. Martin's, 1986: interestingly relates Blake's own background to the poetry)

S. Gardner, *Literature in Perspective: Blake* (Evans, 1988: a very readable general introduction to his life and work)

E. Larrissy, *William Blake* (Blackwell Re-reading Literature Series, 1985: a fine introduction to Marxist criticism)

D. Lindsey, *Songs of Innocence and Experience* (Macmillan Critics Debate Series, 1989: a fascinatingly useful critical survey of the full range of interpretive possibilities allied to a close reading of selected poems)

K. Raine, *William Blake* (Thames and Hudson World of Art Library Series, 1970: an invaluable introduction to Blake's paintings and engravings, lavishly illustrated and relating the art closely to the poetry and mystical philosophy)

K. Raine, *Golgonooza, City of Imagination; Last Studies in William Blake* (Golgonooza Press, 1991: an accessible book, emphasising the mystical interpretation of Blake)